THE RIGHT WAY TO
KEEP PONIES

Where to find Right Way

Elliot Right Way take pride in our editorial quality, accuracy and value-for-money. Booksellers everywhere can rapidly obtain any Right Way book for you. If you have been particularly pleased with any one title, do please mention this to your bookseller as personal recommendation helps us enormously.

Please send to the address on the back of the title page opposite, a stamped, self-addressed envelope if you would like a copy of our free catalogue. Alternatively, you may wish to browse through our extensive range of informative titles arranged by subject on the Internet at **www.right-way.co.uk**

We welcome views and suggestions from readers as well as from prospective authors; do please write to us or e-mail:
info@right-way.co.uk

THE RIGHT WAY TO KEEP PONIES

Hugh Venables

Illustrated by Christine Bousfield

RIGHT WAY

CONTENTS

PREFACE

At least half, and probably more, of the fun of having ponies comes from looking after them. Today a pony is far more than just a beast of burden, and becomes part of the family just as much as any well-loved dog or cat.

The equine animal is not easy to keep in good health. The days when the job of caring for a horse or pony could easily be left to someone whose business it was are, for most of us, gone for ever. If we wish to ride we must do more than just pay for our mount's housing, feeding and clothing. We have to be prepared to feed it, groom it ourselves, and to clean the stable.

The number of ponies now kept for pleasure is steadily increasing. Many of the people who buy one have had no previous experience of looking after such a large animal, and will have no-one nearby to whom they can turn for reliable advice. You might laugh at the man who tried to feed his horse on meat and dog meal. Nevertheless it is all too easy for the novice to make assumptions which the experienced pony-keeper finds astonishing, simply because the novice does not appreciate how different the pony is from other animals he has dealt with.

A pony is very similar to a horse. For most practical purposes it can be considered as a horse, but in a smaller, hardier version. Care of the pony is the prime concern of this book because most people's first equine experience is usually with a pony, either their own or their children's. But with only slight modification to allow for the greater size and, perhaps, more aristocratic breeding, all that is said about the care of the pony can be applied to the care of the horse.

Much that is written and said about the care of ponies is arguable; some is downright wrong. Experts vary widely in their opinions on any one aspect, though as experience grows, so you realise that one particular routine or method may be no better or worse than another.

The suggestions given in this book are the product of one person's accumulated knowledge and practical experience. As far as possible, reasons for each point have been given. I hope this will help you to remember the right way rather than the wrong, and save you from being encumbered with traditional and sometimes erroneous dogma.

1

A PONY IN THE FAMILY

Whether or not to buy a pony is the big question. The young rider looks forward eagerly to many happy hours caring for a pony; grooming, training, and riding. Parents, however, often anticipate a pony's arrival with less enthusiasm, bearing in mind the cost of keep, and providing the equipment that is needed. For some, too, there is the unpleasant feeling that they know little or nothing about the day-to-day requirements of such a large animal with the added worry of not being able to cope with problems such as illness.

The addition of a pony to the family brings many benefits. Parents find relief from months, perhaps years, of nagging and begging by their horse-mad children. They can feel with confidence that pony-ownership will encourage their offspring to enjoy stimulating and healthy recreation, involving plenty of exercise in the open air. A child's sense of responsibility and a degree of self-control are both developed by caring for a living animal. So too is the ability to accept disappointment, as when a tragedy strikes such as the pony going lame the day before the local gymkhana.

Riding in the country brings the opportunity to watch and learn about agriculture, the way plants and trees grow and the behaviour of wild animals; all much more interesting when seen at first hand than when viewed on television. This, and the pleasure of just being with the pony, make pony-keeping a worthwhile occupation for any young person – and for the not-so-young, too.

Riders of ponies also gain socially, meeting other enthusiasts at local pony shows and Pony Club rallies. Their parents are likely to become involved, too, and many enjoy attending pony-orientated gatherings in a supporting and picnic-basketcarrying role. Most pony events are held in pleasant places; the people are friendly and the social life comes to involve the whole family, not

Fig.1. Riding in the country.

only its riding members. Unfortunately, parents can become too competitive and the pleasant atmosphere is lost as winning becomes all important, though this occurs relatively rarely.

Buying a Pony

Despite strong arguments in favour of acquiring a pony, there are some circumstances under which it is better not to buy one. Getting a pony as a status symbol is foolish as it differs from most other indicators of wealth in being a living creature and requiring constant attention. A pony cannot be ridden occasionally and just turned out in the field when not wanted in the same way as a toy is returned to the cupboard. Under such treatment the animal is likely to become difficult to manage and unreliable. Whether being worked or not, a pony still needs daily feeding and watering, shelter in bad weather, proper attention to the feet, and so on. Neglect of these basics is cruel to the animal and is particularly likely when a pony is bought for a child who does not really want one.

Given that someone is keen to have a pony, is their riding good enough and their knowledge of horses sufficient yet? Though many children long for a pony from a very early age it is probably unwise to buy one until the age of eight or nine. Younger than this, the child is unlikely to be strong enough, or a sufficiently competent rider, to go far off the leading rein, nor will the child be able to make much contribution to looking after the animal.

There is a general tendency to overestimate one's own, and one's children's, capabilities – and this goes for riding as much as anything else. One has to be *taught* to ride properly. Adequate lessons at a good riding school (BHS Approved, for example) are essential before a pony is purchased. The rider must master the elements of equitation and how to cope with the pony *before* it arrives. Hours spent hanging around riding schools and other people's ponies (without being a nuisance, of course) are not entirely wasted, as some of the 'Do's' and 'Don'ts' of handling horses are learned. But as long as there is any doubt about the young rider's confidence and proficiency, it is best to delay acquisition of a pony rather than risk the rider being hurt or frightened.

The cost should be properly estimated in advance, for it is, unfortunately, expensive to keep a pony. Even a 'rough', hardy pony with only the most basic, secondhand equipment, is not cheap to maintain, though relatively inexpensive to buy. Indeed, the purchase price of a pony is usually the least of the problems. Besides providing a field and shelter and food, other expenses crop up; shoeing, for example, and repairs to saddlery; also attention to the field and its fences to keep them in reasonable order. Can you afford the cost of veterinary treatment if the pony becomes seriously ill?

It is said that time and money are interchangeable, but both are needed when you have a pony. Some supervision is needed if young people are to ride safely. They must wear hard hats (conforming to BSI specifications) with chin straps always fastened. When people go riding it is as well to know roughly where they are going and approximately when they intend to be back. If the pony's owner is at boarding school, another member of the family may have to step in and look after the animal; on a cold, dark, winter evening this requires some dedication. The invasion of the house by all the trappings of pony-keeping also demands remarkable tolerance from other members of the family who are not necessarily very enthusiastic about matters equine.

The Mind of the Pony
Ponies differ from most other domestic pets in size and especially in temperament. With experience, handling horses or ponies becomes very easy and the knowledgeable horseman almost seems to read his animals' minds. This understanding grows from thoughtful observation of them, watching what they do and learning why they do it, so that the best horsemen come to anticipate a horse's reaction in any particular circumstance.

It is a help to have a wider understanding of the background of the equine species. Wild ponies live on open grassland; their cousins, the zebras, still do in parts of Africa. On these plains they move about in herds, grazing and wandering perhaps ten miles a day, perhaps twenty, just looking for their natural food, which is grass. Wild ponies are on the move, slowly, for much of the time.

Predatory beasts on the great plains depended on catching the ancestral ponies for food; zebras still have to keep a wary eye open all the time for meat-eaters such as lions. Grass-eating animals instinctively stay together as twenty eyes are better than two. Ponies today still have this herd instinct. The eye-sight of ponies is well developed, particularly for spotting something moving – it could be a lion – a long way off. Ponies' eyes are placed in the sides of their heads, rather than at the front (as human eyes are), so that they can see almost all around their bodies without having to move their heads. (See fig. 2.)

Ponies tend to be nervous and jumpy. Their wild ancestors had to be alert all the time to spot enemies and relied for survival on fast reactions and the ability to flee. The modern pony still has the same automatic reaction to danger, running away. If confined and unable to gallop the pony becomes terrified, often struggling wildly and quite irrationally, making things worse. A really frightened pony becomes difficult to manage and often behaves abnormally as instinct takes over from training. One of the secrets of success in handling ponies lies in anticipating the causes of fear, so that the animal can be kept out of the way or distracted.

All horses and ponies have a very acute sense of hearing. Those mobile ears tell the animal from which direction even small

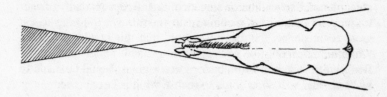

Fig. 2. A pony can see almost all round the body without moving the head. The shaded area is the field of binocular vision (i.e. this area can be seen by both eyes at once).

sounds come. Make use of this when walking up to the pony. If you talk, then the pony knows where you are, and you don't 'pop up' unexpectedly. This gives the pony confidence, particularly when your voice is familiar. When out riding, notice how the pony flicks back an ear to listen if you speak. After a while, most ponies can be taught to respond to a few verbal commands: 'Walk', 'Trot', 'Stand', and so on. These must always be the same words, and, very importantly, said in the same tone of voice. Don't forget that a pony is sensitive to, and will be upset by, strange sounds; these include loud talking or shouting, which never serve any useful purpose with ponies and can do a lot of harm.

Alertness, acute hearing and good sight are features of ponies, but why else do they sometimes behave apparently quite inexplicably? The pony differs from humans and, to some extent, from animals like dogs, in having a very good memory but little logic. All training is therefore achieved by the same system of responses to a particular command, followed by reward. As you ride, you do this by applying an 'aid' or instruction in the form, for example, of pressure on the left rein for a left turn. When the pony responds, and turns, you release the pressure, and this is the reward. The pony does not like the feel of the bit pulled, even if gently, against the side of the mouth. From past experience, the pony knows to turn, and then the uncomfortable feeling will stop. Of course, it would be just as easy to throw the rider, and gallop off into the distance. Fortunately ponies are not usually intelligent enough to work that out, nor do they realise their own strength; such behaviour is not in their nature.

Always be absolutely consistent with the pony. Even the simplest matter, like leading on a headcollar and rope, is really further training. If the animal is allowed to misbehave, loitering to eat grass for instance, the idea takes hold that this is all right. Such wrongdoings should be corrected immediately, often just with a sharp word. The pony which stops to eat grass should be made to walk on, and will soon come to realise what is not allowed.

In correcting a pony, firmness, not brutality, is needed. There is no point in trying to hurt or frighten. This only makes a pony nervous and difficult to handle; it will remember the whole incident as a nasty experience, but will not know why. Determination, on your part, is important though, and generally it is you who should decide what the pony is to do, and get him to do it. However, this should not involve a battle royal and if occasionally you find that you have asked too much, then it is better to give in than try to fight it out. Absolute confidence is essential in riding and handling ponies; they have an astonishing ability to sense human nervousness and exploit it.

Approaching the Pony
A few words of greeting to the pony are helpful at any time, and will ensure that a dozing animal is not frightened by your creeping up unnoticed. Always approach from the front, because otherwise the pony could kick out with the hind legs. Approach slowly and quietly; if you bound up shouting and laughing, the pony may begin to wonder what on earth this thing is, and with good reason!

Ponies' skins are sensitive, and they find very light handling ticklish, so always stroke or pat gently but firmly. Most ponies and horses, once they have had a look at you, seem to enjoy a pat on the neck, though they dislike being patted on the face, and can you really blame them? Handling the head has to be done with some care, moving slowly and deliberately so that you don't startle the pony, and being particularly careful about touching the ears. Some animals resent this very much.

Ponies differ from other animals which might be kept as pets, such as dogs and cats. They don't seem to enjoy being stroked for its own sake; rather they tolerate it in the hope that a tit-bit might appear. Favoured tit-bits are dry crusts of bread or toast, strong peppermints, and carrots; the carrots should be cut lengthways into thick fingers because if they are sliced into rounds there is a chance that a greedy pony could swallow one whole and choke on it. Apples are also enjoyed by ponies, in a rather dribbly way. These, too, should be cut into long pieces.

Horses and ponies are traditionally offered lumps of sugar, but I do not recommend this. The reason is not that sugar damages a pony's teeth (unlikely unless you give it by the hundredweight) but because ponies are often too fond of it and seem to become almost addicted. The result is that a pony can become very naughty, nipping and even kicking with eagerness for another lump. Too much of any tit-bit can spoil a pony, of course, but none so fast as sugar.

When you give a tit-bit, always offer it with your hand flat, so that the pony can pick up the delicacy without taking your fingers as well. In giving tit-bits try to avoid the development of naughty tricks like nipping, and never encourage this by letting the pony search your pockets for bits. The best behaviour results from tit-bits coming only on well-defined occasions. When you go to the pony in the field, and when it is turned out again are good times

Fig 3. Always offer a tit-bit with your hand flat.

to give a delicacy and this will make catching easier. An occasional tit-bit if the pony does well in training, for example, is also a useful way of indicating your pleasure. But if you want to give your pony a special treat it is better to make up a really delicious feed than to give a lot of tit-bits by hand.

2

WHERE TO KEEP THE PONY?

Before you buy, here is the first problem you must face. Where are you going to keep the pony?

In summer there may be little difficulty; almost any animal will live out, day and night. Winter is another matter.

Whatever the time of year, don't forget that a pony, being a large animal, eats a considerable bulk of food every day. This applies whether grazing, living on hay and 'concentrates' (grain-based food), or a bit of both. A half-acre orchard for example will not be able to provide enough grass for even one pony all through the year. Moreover, those hard hooves, whether shod or not, can cut up a small paddock very badly. You may find the 'grazing' is soon turned into a morass, with the dejected animal standing in the middle of it, fetlock deep in mud.

If you have only a small area in which to keep the pony then you may be able to rent extra grazing land not too far from home. Alternatively, wear and tear on the field can be reduced by keeping the pony in a stable for part of the time. This will mean you need extra hay and concentrates, the amount depending on the pony's size, the amount of work, and how much grass is available from the paddock.

One-and-a-half to two acres of reasonable quality grazing is the minimum required for a pony that is to live 'out' on a diet based on grass. It is frequently asserted that a pony can live outside all year round, requiring no shelter from cold winds, rain or snow in winter, nor from flies in the summer. And it is certainly true that wild ponies of the 'Mountain and Moorland' breeds – Exmoor, Dartmoor, Shetland, Highland, Fell, Dale, New Forest, Welsh Mountain and Connemara – survive some very hard winters with no shelter at all. But the important word is *survive*, not thrive, and these ponies are not expected to work, even at weekends. More importantly, they have very large areas of land over which to roam in search of food and where they have more chance of finding shelter behind rocks or trees. This is very different from the unfortunate animal enclosed in a small, bare paddock. It has been rightly suggested that the life of a pony is shortened by the need to survive the rigours of a British winter out of doors. Even more supplementary feeding will he needed for the pony which is 'out' all the time without shelter.

So, though you may plan that your pony should, basically, lead an outdoor life – and most ponies are best kept thus – you should acknowledge the need for some sort of simple building. It need only be a shelter made with walls of straw bales and a roof of corrugated iron, but it must provide somewhere to get out of the wind and let the coat dry. The shelter should also have a hard floor to

Fig. 4. . . . the unfortunate pony in a small, bare paddock.

enable the animal to stand on a dry surface. Preferably it should be bedded down to provide a resting-place for a few hours each day.

Contrary to common belief, horses and ponies *do* lie down if they have somewhere reasonably comfortable to do so – well, would you settle down for a snooze in four inches of freezing mud? On those mild days in early spring it is obvious how much ponies appreciate a chance to rest, for they will often lie stretched out, as dead, in the warm sunshine.

Most ponies are in the habit of lying down for a few hours during the night or early morning in summer, though you may not see them doing it. Of course, equines can also doze standing up, and many get much of their sleep in that way. In winter, outdoor ponies will seldom lie down and rest at night, partly because there is nowhere warm and dry to lie and partly because at night it may be so cold that they have to walk around to keep warm. For this reason, any lying down is done during the warmest part of the day, around noon, when you are about. You may gain the false impression that the pony lies down to sleep more in winter than in summer.

Keeping a Pony 'At Grass'
The easiest method of keeping a pony, and the most economical in labour and cost, is in a paddock with a shelter or stable into which the animal can go at will. Under this system, less work devolves on the keeper, who has only to go and look the pony over once a day, check the water, provide the food, and keep the shelter bedded down, cleaning it out from time to time.

Loose in the field the pony will not require daily exercise as would be needed if confined to a stable; wandering about keeps the animal moderately fit and prevents an unpleasant excess of energy when it is time to be ridden. Freedom to graze or rest is a more natural life than that of the stabled animal, and ponies so kept are generally more healthy. Some animals, those with more Thoroughbred or Arab in them, are not really hardy enough to live out, however, and need to be more cosseted and stabled at night during winter.

There are snags to keeping a pony out of doors all the time. One is that the animal may be wet and dirty when you want to ride. In winter, particularly, the shaggy coat gets very muddy when the pony rolls about and it is hard to get it clean. Outdoor ponies never look very smart at this time of year. A pony kept at grass can become remarkably fit in summer with plenty of exercise. In winter, however, the heavy winter coat causes excessive sweating so

Fig. 5. The shaggy coat gets very muddy when the pony rolls.

that little fast work can be done. On the other hand there is a saving in cost as no rugs are required. Further, being free to graze all the time (as long as there is something on the field) the pony requires relatively less supplementary feeding in winter, though some will always be needed.

The 'Half-and-Half' System
A modification of the 'at grass' method described above, the 'half-and-half' system, involves stabling the pony by day in summer but by night in winter. The rest of the time is spent turned out in the field. This follows the animal's natural inclinations, as in summer most ponies prefer to be inside during the day, when they get relief from the pestering flies, and in winter they shelter at night when it is coldest.

The 'half-and-half' system also gives the rider the best of both worlds in summer, for the pony is in and ready to ride during the day; at night both sustenance and exercise are taken! Stabling for part of the time during the summer also allows you to restrict the amount of lush grass which is eaten, an important matter with ponies, otherwise they can easily become too stout. The system is not quite so convenient in winter, with the pony out by day and stabled at night. The animal is not always standing ready to be ridden. This is not very important, as riders are usually occupied with school or work for most of the daylight hours in winter. In fact, the 'half-and-half' system of pony-keeping can suit most people quite well, as the animal requires attention only first thing in the morning and then again in the evening.

Of course, there is rather more work involved in keeping a pony this way, compared with being 'at grass'. The animal has to be turned out and brought in, the stable requires daily cleaning and bedding down, the water bucket replenishing, and in winter, two feeds a day will be required. Also, because more time is spent in it, the stabling itself has to be rather superior. It must be equipped with a door, and window for ventilation, rather than relying on a wide entrance (perhaps closed with a rail) as a field shelter does.

Kept in at night in winter, the pony can be partially clipped, and removal of that heavy coat will make faster work possible. It will also necessitate the wearing of rugs to keep warm: a waterproof 'New Zealand' one when outside and a quilted or similar stable rug when inside. Changing the rugs also adds to the work of keeping the pony. Though out for only a relatively small proportion of the time, the pony will require almost as much hay and concentrates as the animal which is stabled all the time, though there is less need for exercise and grooming.

The Stabled Pony
A pony may be kept in a loose box (or stall) day and night, but will require considerable attention to be kept fit and occupied. On the other hand, such a pony is ready to be ridden at virtually any time and is able to do hard, fast work. But an animal as fit as this may become rather full of energy at times, and requires a capable rider.

The stabled pony requires about two hours' exercise a day. The movement is essential for health as it stimulates digestion, improves circulation and removal of waste gases from the body. Particularly important, it improves the blood flow to the feet and limbs. The daily work also keeps the pony fit and prevents boredom. Regular grooming is required, as is feeding three or four times a day, and the stable will require frequent attention. All of this is too much to be fitted around school or some other full-time occupation.

It requires considerable skills and experience to keep a stabled pony in good condition, fit but not unmanageable. The stabled way of life is quite unnatural and the diet artificial. Even if you do all the work yourself it is more expensive to keep a pony in all the time in terms of feed and bedding, shoeing and rugs. Well-designed stabling with an adequate storage area is particularly important when so much work is done there.

The Decision
Of the three systems described, the most popular, and probably the best for small ponies, is one where the animal is turned out all the time, with a shelter which can be used when desired. The pony can be shut in if necessary, for the night before a gymkhana or hunting, for example, and can be enclosed in summer if excessive amounts of grass are being eaten. For young riders, the grass-fed pony has the distinct advantage that any spare energy is expended in grazing rather than in mischief, as it might be if the food came in a bucket. From the point of view of parents, a pony which is at grass requires minimum attention, and the hardy type is usually self-sufficient most of the time.

For the larger pony which may be expected to hunt during the winter, the half-and-half system allows reasonable fitness to be maintained, without any build-up of excessive energy. It is also a suitable method for keeping a better-bred animal. Stabling ponies all the time – and horses as well, for that matter – is best avoided unless they are to be worked very hard, as they can so easily get out of hand. This happens more often than people realise. The result in these instances is that much of the pleasure of owning a pony can be lost as the rider may not always be sure that he is in control of the animal.

3

THE PONY'S FIELD

Wandering around the field foraging will keep a pony healthy. This is far closer to the natural way of life than is standing cooped up in a stable all day, waiting for food to be brought 'on a plate' or, rather, in a bucket. However, keeping your pony in a field requires first that you have, or you can find, a suitable pony-proof field.

If you or your family have a sizeable paddock of your own, the problem is not likely to be too great. Do not over-estimate the ability of a pocket-handkerchief of ground to support one or more ponies. Between one and a half and two acres of grazing per pony is a minimum. On less than this do not be surprised when all the edible grass disappears and the animals require considerable quantities of other food, hay and concentrates, to be brought to them throughout the year. It is also easy to underestimate how much *damage* horses or ponies can do to grassland. Their feet wear large bare and muddy patches round troughs, shelter entrances, gateways and other favourite standing places.

If you have only a small paddock of your own, you may need to 'rest' it every few months to let the grass recover while the pony is grazed somewhere else. Since rented grazing may be some distance away it is sensible to try to arrange for your pony to take these 'holidays' during term time, or when your work is at its busiest. But even if there is no field near home where you can graze a pony, it is still possible to keep one, though, of course, it is less convenient.

Fencing
This is a particular problem with rented land. Fencing may be inadequate and sometimes you may have to reject a field where the fences are in a very poor condition. Where you are using a

paddock on a long term basis, stout fences and proper repairs are a good investment They will last better and you will be able to enjoy the peace of mind that comes from knowing that your pony is securely enclosed.

The ideal type of fencing for horses is wooden post and rail erected inside existing hedges. This may be rather expensive though, and requires considerable maintenance to keep it in good order. It is seldom feasible for the average pony-keeper. A thick well-kept hedge, with or without a ditch, is generally sufficient to prevent most ponies from escaping. This also requires attention, and cutting of the hedge each autumn so that it grows thick and not straggly.

Hedges should be examined at intervals for the appearance of thin places – incipient gaps which will require fortifying with posts and rails, or posts and strained wire. Though ponies do not barge through hedges and fences as much as cattle do, they will nonetheless make use of any gaps they can find. They have all day to wander round looking for weak places; and the grass is always *so* much greener on the other side . . .

Dry stone walls, kept in good repair, provide good fencing for ponies' fields. Like a thick hedge, a wall can provide welcome shelter from wind and driving rain. High banks may serve to keep ponies in, though all equines are athletic. Banks of rivers and streams may tempt ponies to explore further unless the obstacles are either quite imposing in themselves, or made so by the presence of another fence on the inward side.

So much for what might be termed 'permanent' fences; we must also consider the type that you can put up yourself. Cheaper alternatives to wooden post and rail include posts interspaced with plain wire, or with rubber or PVC strands, or with mesh netting (preferably intended for horses).

These must be strained tight; and special tools and some strength are required. Such fences are best put up by a professional, but they may not be beyond the capabilities of the average family handyman. If such fencing is not drawn tight, it can be very dangerous because ponies can so easily get themselves tangled in it and, once caught, they struggle and can injure themselves quite badly.

Even with a properly erected wire fence the lowest strand

should be a minimum of 1–1½ ft (30–45cm) above the ground. Thick wire is less likely than thin to become caught behind the heels of an animal's shoes, as well as being more easily visible. Barbed wire is not recommended for ponies. Nasty injuries can occur when a pony gets its foot caught in loose wire. If a rented field is fenced with barbed wire, it is essential to ensure that it is kept taut at all times.

Before turning a pony into a new field, time spent on checking fences for hazards is never wasted; spare ends of wire should be cut off with wire cutters, or secured out of the way with staples.

Some sorts of fencing are unsuitable for ponies and should be avoided whenever possible. Chestnut paling is such a type as it tends to be flimsy and, again, it is easy for an animal to be caught up in it. The old bedsteads and parts of wrecked motor cars that

Fig. 6. Show the electric fence to the pony when it is newly installed.

are sometimes used to fill gaps cannot be recommended either. For filling gaps in an emergency there is much to be said for the electric fence, which is readily portable, easy to erect, and is well respected. Most ponies, once they have had one shock from it, have only to hear the tick of the battery unit to make them keep well clear of the wire. It has the disadvantage that it may not be clearly visible, so it is necessary to show the fence to the pony when it is newly installed. This is particularly important if the electric fence is being used to divide a paddock in half as when, for example, one part is being rested or has been spread with weedkiller.

Gateways
The ideal way of filling the gateway into a field is with a gate, preferably one that swings easily, opens wide and has an effective fastening – not a piece of string or twisted wire. Some ponies become very clever at undoing even proper gate catches and you may find that as a safety measure an additional fastening of the

Fig. 7. Slip-rails fixed by passing a U-shaped peg through one end.

snap-on (like a big dog-lead catch) type, or toggle and ring, is necessary. Fortunately, ponies cannot undo a padlock and chain, nor can picnickers or vandals.

Slip-rails are an alternative that is considerably cheaper than a gate, and they are as effective and almost as convenient. Metal loops are used, with either round or sawn rails passing through them. The rails may be secured, if necessary, by drilling holes through each rail and passing a U-shaped peg through one end (see fig. 7). As a purely temporary measure, small stones jammed between rail and loop will often prevent animals from getting the rails down. Wire gateways are dangerous and should not be used for horses.

As a general rule fences which are cattle proof are also pony proof, though few cattle are such good jumpers as ponies. The stretches of fence in a pony's field which are likely to come in for most abuse are those around the gateway, where the animals assemble at feeding times, and fences separating them from other horses. Ponies will lean over hedges and gates to 'talk'

Fig. 8. Wire gateways are dangerous. The wire tends to slacken and is liable to cause injury.

to their friends on the other side, sometimes with unfortunate results, the fences either giving way or entangling the animals as they paw and stamp.

Ponies that Get Out
Ponies generally escape for a good reason. One is that, as far as the animal is concerned, the gap is there, so why not make use of it? Things always look better outside. Regular checks on all the field's fences are most important, in particular those fences which would allow ponies to stray onto roads.

Loose animals are a serious danger to themselves in modern traffic and can also cause nasty accidents, for which their owner may be liable. Claims arising from such incidents can be very large and the premiums are relatively small, so that it is really essential to take out some sort of Public Liability insurance if you keep horses or ponies.

Even if you have checked all the fences thoroughly you may find that there are still attempts to escape. You should try to find the reason for this and ask yourself: is the pony getting enough to eat, or being driven by hunger to look elsewhere for food? A pony may also get out because of loneliness. Horses are naturally gregarious animals and some seem to find great hardship in being alone for long periods. Another pony is the ideal companion, but a donkey, or even some cows, will often be a settling influence.

There are a few ponies which seem to delight in getting out for the sake of it, and may even jump back into their own field when they have had enough of the outside world. They seem to see each fence as a challenge to their jumping – or scrambling – ability, though such animals are rare. This foible has to be accepted, for unless you can find a field with colossal fences there is little that can be done to prevent their getting out, beyond ensuring that they have equine companions, enough food and water and sufficient work to use up spare time and energy.

Other Hazards
Before putting your pony into a field here are some dangers you should look for apart from those in the fences. Bits of old farm machinery, heaps of rubbish, or the odd broken bottle can all

cause serious injuries and should be cleared away or fenced off. If
you cannot do this at least try to make the hazard as safe as possible by removing potential traps and sharp projections.

Ponies are, fortunately, basically sensible. They will usually
cope very well with rough ground in their field, unless they are
driven over it fast. Even then, once they know the terrain they will
usually find their way amazingly cleverly. But if you know that
there are large numbers of rabbit holes or the like in a new field,
it is best to prevent the pony from tearing wildly round it when
first turned out. This excited galloping is never a good thing as
animals may also charge into fences. It can be discouraged by giving ponies a hard day's work before they go into the strange field,
and not too much to eat for about six hours before being turned
out. The first thought is then 'Food!'. The pony will get down to
the business of grazing at once, and leave exploring until after a
good meal.

Inter-pony Relationships
All horses and ponies prefer companionship to loneliness. But,
paradoxically, they may seem to fight viciously on being first
introduced to one another, so owners may be worried by the
prospect of turning out strange ponies together. The best approach
is really to let the animals sort things out among themselves,
preferably with plenty of space in which to do it. They seldom
injure one another deliberately. Accidents are most likely to occur
as a result of a pony not looking where it is going and running into
a fence. Obviously an animal that is known to be vicious (and
such are very rare) is better kept separate.

It is best to introduce the strangers in a completely new field,
where none has any prior claim to the premises. They can be
expected to sniff each other and squeal and gallop round for a
while. This is worrying for the human onlookers but apparently
thoroughly enjoyed by the participants, as is the play-biting and
high-kicking. If you are worried about the risks of kicks, injuries
are minimised by having the ponies' hind shoes removed until
they have settled down, usually in a few days.

When ponies live in a group they usually establish their own
special friendships and particular animals become bosses. Care
has to be taken when extra food is being given that there is no

bullying of the less powerful characters (not necessarily the smallest in size) and that each animal gets a fair share; heaps or nets of hay, for example, should be set far enough apart for no one pony to be able to monopolise two portions.

Water
Whether your pony is in the field or the stable, a plentiful supply of clean fresh water, available at all times, is essential. In the field a natural spring may be used, provided it is easily accessible and not surrounded by too much mud, and you should check that it does not dry up in hot weather. The same applies if your pony relies on a pond or stream for drinking water.

The automatically filled water trough is convenient, generally reliable, and does not dry up in summer, though it may freeze solid in very cold weather. A glance every so often will ensure that it is full to the correct level and that the ball valve that shuts off the supply when the trough is full has not stuck, allowing the water to overflow. Not only does this waste water, it also makes the area round the trough very muddy. Because a certain amount of spillage is inevitable from any water trough, and because animals are continually going to it, it should if possible be placed on a high, dry part of the field, preferably on a hard standing.

If a concrete or galvanised iron field trough is not available it may be possible to press an old bath into service as a water container. The enamelled, full-size variety requires something more permanent than a rubber bath plug to block the plughole. A concrete or a wooden bung is best. The undersides of the edges of most baths are rather sharp and wooden boxing may be needed to prevent the pony's knees being cut on them (see fig. 9). A cover is also necessary to protect a ball valve or tap from the pony's attentions, to prevent injury and to avoid catching the headcollar.

A small metal tub or a couple of big buckets can be used to hold the pony's water, but these have the disadvantage that they are easily tipped up. If you are considering carrying your pony's daily water supply you should estimate a requirement in the region of 8 gallons (37 litres) a day. Considerably more than this could be wanted for hard work or if the weather is very hot.

The water itself should always be clean (would you like to drink dirty water?) and all troughs require emptying and scrub-

Fig. 9. If an old bath is pressed into service, the sides may need to be boxed in with wood.

bing out periodically. A pony should never be left without water even for a few hours. Not only is it essential for the digestion, and indeed for life, but if a pony is allowed to get very thirsty it will gulp down large quantities of water when it is offered once again, which can cause digestive problems such as colic. To deprive any animal of water is also very unkind. When one can go to the tap and get a drink of water at any time it is perhaps hard to envisage finding, one day, that it has run dry. But this is how the thirsty animal feels on going to the water trough and finding it empty.

4

HOUSING FOR A PONY

Pony accommodation can range from the smart and expensive stable yard, complete with tack room and feed stores, garaging for the horse box and – of course – the stable cat, to the simplest of field shelters. It need not be costly and elaborate, however, and very useful stabling can be made by altering a variety of existing buildings. Garden sheds, garages, summer houses, calf pens, barns, nissen huts and even cart shelters have been used, though some – such as greenhouses – have to be rejected. Alternatively, a building may be put up specially, and here again there are a number of possibilities, depending on financial resources, and the ingenuity of the builder.

Before starting to construct the stable it is as well to consider just what is wanted. A pony can be housed in either a loose box or a stall. In the box there is freedom to move about at pleasure in what is, effectively, a square or rectangular room. In a stall, less popular nowadays for housing horses, the animal is tied head to the wall, and there is a passage behind the stall. If you are using a building which was not designed as stabling, it may be easier to provide a stall than a loose box, particularly where the place is used only on a temporary basis.

A stall is about 6 feet (1.8 metres) wide and, from the front wall, about 11 feet (3.3 metres) long. There is a passage of some 8 feet (2.4 metres) behind it. The total floor area is about the same as that of a loose box, which would be from 10–12 feet by 10 feet (about 3.5 metres by 3 metres) – that is just over 100 square feet (9 square metres). The roof height in the stable should be sufficient to ensure that the pony does not bang its head on the ceiling or the roof beams; about 10 feet (3 metres) or more is desirable. If the stable is too low, the volume of air is reduced and it may become hot and stuffy. This is unlikely to be a problem where one side of the building is open or closed only with rails, as with many field shelters.

Walls and Roofs

Brick or concrete block walls are probably ideal as they are completely windproof and are good insulators. This is particularly noticeable in summer when brick stables remain pleasantly cool. These materials are also very long lasting, and are proof against the kicking of most animals. The cost of constructing a stable of brick may be prohibitive, but a conversion may be feasible. Brick walls have an advantage in that they are easily painted and even the tattiest of buildings can be made to look quite smart. The inside of stables is traditionally painted with a black washable paint – often bituminous – to a height of some 3½–4 feet (1–1.2

Fig. 10. In a stall, the pony is tied head to the wall. The pony is secured by a headrope running through a loop to a wooden 'log' so that spare rope is not allowed to hang down where it might tangle the feet.

metres) – that is as high as it is likely to be soiled. Above that, limewash or emulsion paint in white or some other light colour is usual. When painting stabling it is well to remember that horses and ponies may find that they have nothing better to do than lick the paintwork, so use paints which are recommended for use in livestock buildings.

Perhaps the most popular sort of stabling being built today is the sectional wooden type, which is stoutly made. The sections have only to be bolted together on a suitable base to provide almost 'instant stabling', with very little effort for the purchaser. A number of manufacturers make these buildings and they are a simple, quick and effective way of housing a pony. Additions can also be made very easily to the original structure, as most of the buildings are designed with this possibility in mind.

With timber buildings there is a risk that a pony may be able to kick through a thin wall, not only making a hole in the wall but possibly injuring the foot too. Most pre-fabricated stables are lined with strong boards to above kicking height to prevent this from happening, but if you plan to use some other wooden building, remember this risk. If heavy sawn planks are too costly it may be possible to use off-cut planks, the outermost planks sawn from a tree, which have bark on one side. Though not beautiful these are solid, and usually reasonably cheap.

Building a simple stable or shelter from scratch need not be very difficult. But compare your estimated cost with that of a pre-fabricated building before you start; it may not be very different. An economical structure can be made using a timber frame with heavy off-cut planks nailed to the outside of it. Lined with boards or roofing felt and with a roof of corrugated iron, this will make a surprisingly good stable. Though it would never be called decorative, if the work is properly done it can look quite neat.

A rough alternative, rather temporary but better than nothing, is to use iron roofing, supported on a wooden frame with walls of straw bales. The bales should be fixed to the frame to ensure that they do not collapse. Since ventilation in such buildings may be minimal they are generally best with only three or three and a half walls, leaving a wide entrance.

Straw bales may also be useful if you are converting another building to provide accommodation for your pony. They can be

used to line draughty walls or, with a stout rail, to block a spare
doorway. At all times the bales should be strongly secured to prevent them from falling down. They may need to be protected from
the pony's attentions (in particular from being eaten) by rails or a
gate. Rails, with or without straw bales behind them to protect
from draughts, are useful if you want to partition off part of a
bigger building to house the pony. They need to be of sufficient
height to prevent the pony jumping them, that is, with a top rail
about 4–5 feet (1.5 metres) above the ground, depending on the
size of the pony. Middle and lower rails are best spaced between
1 and 1½ feet (just under half a metre) apart. There is little point
in having the bottom bar below about 18 inches (45cm) from the
ground; the pony is unlikely to get under it. If whoever uses the
rest of the building would rather it were kept free of straw, a board
6 inches – 1 foot (15–30cm) wide along the ground below the partition should contain the bedding.

When ponies are used to one another, rails may be enough to
keep them apart. Generally, however, partitions between animals
should be solid, either to the ceiling or effectively so; that is about
6 or 7 feet (2 metres) high. Otherwise, the partition can be boarded
for the bottom 4 feet (1.2 metres) with horizontal or closer vertical rails above. This prevents fighting and kicking as the animals
cannot touch each other. In stalls, partitions are usually high
enough at the front end to prevent the animals seeing one another,
though at the back they are lower, high enough only to prevent
kicking.

Tile or slate roofs are best for stables, but these are expensive
if you are building a stable, and are more common on old barns or
converted buildings. These materials are good insulators and, like
brick walls, keep a stable noticeably cooler in summer. Since most
tile and slate roofs are of a high ridge pattern, they usually provide
a greater volume of air for the animal. Sectional stables quite
often have roofs of wood and waterproof felt – effective materials
– as are the cedar shingles which may be used as an attractive
alternative on such stabling.

Corrugated iron has the advantage of being cheap. It is easy to
manage because it is light, though the ability of its sharp edges to
inflict nasty injuries should not be under-estimated. It tends to
make a building hot in summer and cold in winter unless it is lined

with wooden boarding. The wood also reduces the machine-gun effect of hail on the roof, though most ponies become accustomed to this noise surprisingly quickly.

Doors and Doorways
If there is any choice in the matter it is best if the stable does not face into cold winds and in most parts of Britain a southerly aspect is to be preferred. The front of the stable should not be over-shadowed, by large trees or other buildings for example, so that its supply of air and light is not reduced.

The doorway should be some 6–8 feet (2 metres) high, depending on the size of the pony, which can otherwise get a nasty crack on the head on the top of the door frame. This develops the habit of rushing through the doorway. To avoid banging the pony's hips on the door frame, or the animal's squeezing or treading on the owner when being led out, the doorway should be about 4 feet (1.2 metres) wide. The door itself need be no bigger than is necessary to fill the lower half of the doorway, to a height of some 3 feet 6 inches (about 1 metre) for an average pony of 13.2 HH. The upper half of the door is not really needed as it should never be shut. The doorway provides important ventilation, as well as allowing the pony to look out and see what is going on. There may be fears that the pony might try to jump the lower door. If so, put in a bar, hinged at one end and fastening with a bolt at the other, or simply passed through metal loops like any other slip rail. This provides a simple, cheap and effective means of filling the upper half of the doorway without reducing the ventilation.

The door should open outwards and swing right open, preferably with a hook to fasten it back when the stable is not in use. Since the pony is likely to lean on it, strong hinges with long arms are necessary to prevent the door sagging and becoming difficult to open. It needs to be strongly made, too, for many animals have the trick of banging it with a front foot when impatient, as at feeding time. In doing this a pony would be particularly liable to injury on any sharp edges or projections which might be present on the inside of the door.

Door catches need to be of a type which will stand a lot of wear and tear. They should have no sharp edges which could injure the fingers of the human user, nor any projections which might catch the pony's headcollar. Bolts are very good, particularly those specially made for stables with a loop and catch arrangement. A snap clip can be put through the loop and this will deter even the most skilful pony from undoing it. A kick catch is also very useful (see fig. 11), especially when you are carrying full buckets of water or nets of hay. Being placed near the ground, this type of catch is also out of the pony's reach.

The doorway of a pony's field shelter may be considerably bigger than normal door size. Where several animals share a shed it is essential that the entrance should be wide enough to prevent one pony trapping another inside. It is ideal to have almost the whole of one side (preferably the south side) open. Even if the shelter is only for one pony there is much to be said for leaving one side completely open as this provides plenty of fresh air without risk of cross-draughts. Ponies are seldom bothered by cold, though draughts may cause chilling. An outdoor pony, used to outside temperatures, will be quite happy in an open-sided building. Such a shelter can be enclosed with rails across the entrance should you want to keep the pony in occasionally.

Fig. 11. Door catches: a stable bolt and a 'kick catch'

Windows and Lighting

THE IMPORTANCE OF ADEQUATE VENTILATION CANNOT BE OVERSTRESSED. Animals continuously use up the oxygen in the air and breathe out the gas carbon dioxide. This plus the ammonia produced by decomposing excreta can make the atmosphere 'stuffy' and unhealthy, unless there is sufficient fresh air entering the building. If ventilation is inadequate, there is also a danger that mould spores from hay or straw may build up to dangerous levels and cause lung damage (COPD see page 147) in ponies that are allergic to them.

Windows are one of the best means of ventilation. The sort that is hinged at its lower edge is the best. The sloping pane admits fresh air which mixes with that in the rest of the stable and produces no draught. Most other types of window are less suitable but are nonetheless a good deal better than nothing. The window itself should really be above the animal's head, as in stabling built during the Victorian period. If set lower, it should be barred to prevent the pony from breaking the window and being injured on the broken glass.

There cannot be too much daylight in a stable – another reason for having a window in the building, provided the glass is kept clean. Daylight hours are restricted so it is very helpful to have electric lighting in the stable so that you don't have to attend to the pony at night by light of a torch. On the other hand, faulty electrical wiring is one of the commonest causes of fire so the job of installing the lighting should only be carried out by a qualified electrician.

Light bulbs should be well out of reach of the pony and protected by wire cages to prevent wisps of hay or straw contacting the hot glass. However, the bulbs should not be so far out of reach that it is impossible to change them when they 'pop', as they all do sometime! Wiring should be of the heavy duty type, and, if there is any doubt about the safety of old wiring, it is better replaced or disconnected. Like the rest of the electrical installation, the switches should be where the pony cannot investigate them. The waterproof outdoor models are generally safer and longer-lasting than the ordinary domestic type, though a little more expensive.

5

FLOORS AND THE PONY'S BED

Standing on a bare, cold, wet floor all day is not good for anyone. The same goes for ponies. A clean, dry bed of straw protects them from draughts round the legs, provides something soft for the ponies to stand on while they are inside, and helps to keep the stable smelling pleasant. A pony also needs to lie down for some hours each day to obtain adequate rest, and a clean straw bed will encourage this. A good bed prevents injury, especially to the

Fig. 12. A clean straw bed will encourage the pony to lie down.

hocks and elbows, on the floor or walls as the pony lies down, and it keeps the animal clean.

The bedding is important, too, in that it keeps the stable floor dry. The feet of a pony which has to stand continually in a mixture of dung and urine are likely to suffer badly from such troubles as 'thrush', a smelly, purulent disease of the frog of the foot, which can make a pony very lame.

Flooring

How good a bed one can provide for the pony depends to some extent on the sort of floor on which it is to be made. Putting a proper floor in a stable or shelter can sometimes be almost as expensive as putting up the building itself. There are several alternatives as far as flooring is concerned varying in cost, trouble to put down and effectiveness. The floor of the stable should, ideally, be hard, and of a sort that is easy to clean and which dries quickly – preferably sloped so that it drains adequately. Moreover, it should not be so slippery that animals or people have difficulty in standing up on it, nor should it be so rough that cleaning becomes impossible.

All this sounds like quite a tall order, but in fact concrete makes a very good and reasonably inexpensive material. Once the earth has been dug out to make room for it, it is fairly easy to lay, particularly if bought ready-mixed. It is best put on a layer of rubble or some other hard-core material and a four-inch depth of concrete is required, with a slope of between one in sixty and one in thirty to help it drain. The drain itself is best put outside the stable or in one corner of it rather than in the middle of the floor. If possible, the floor should be a little higher than the surrounding ground, so that no water can seep in from outside.

A concrete 'scree' surface is waterproof and hard, and, if levelled with a board while still wet, is not too slippery. Alternatively, grooves can be drawn in the soft concrete to prevent slipping, though the floor should always be covered with bedding as an additional safe-guard. A paving material may be laid on the concrete base. The old-fashioned vitrified stable bricks with characteristic patterns on them certainly look very smart, are waterproof and wear well. However they require some effort to keep them clean, and are hard to obtain now.

It is possible to produce a quite passable makeshift floor by simply laying bricks, either vitrified or ordinary builder's bricks, on an earth base. The earth should not be too heavy, as it must drain naturally. With this type of flooring urine has to soak away between the bricks. A simple brick floor is constructed with far less effort than a concrete one, though of course it is not as dry nor as long-lasting; however it can be swept clean, if not hosed down, and it is preferable to a bare earth floor.

Many shelters have no special flooring, and the earth, protected from the rain by the roof and stamped hard by the ponies, often remains surprisingly dry. The success of the bare earth floor depends to some extent on the soil type of the area, and on the situation of the stable. Marshy sites are best avoided.

It also depends on how much one intends to shut the pony in. At the best of times ponies can hardly be said to be house-trained and it is surprising how much urine and dung one animal can produce in a night. Well trampled on, this can reduce a dry earth floor to a wet, muddy puddle in a very short time. If an earth floor is all that is available, you may well find that a 'deep litter' system of bedding down is more successful than one where the stable is completely mucked out each day.

Types of Bedding Material
Traditionally, wheat straw is considered the ideal bedding material, although in practice barley straw is as suitable. Straw of either type should be dry, free from mould and blackness, and a light golden colour, when bought. It should look and smell pleasant. If the straw has only been lightly crushed during harvesting it will not absorb urine so readily and will be more economical as only a small amount will have to be discarded each day because it is sodden. But, modern methods of harvesting allow for little variation in this.

Barley straw was not considered to be as good as wheat because the long barley hairs could irritate the skin of thin-skinned horses. In practice, this is not important for ponies. These mainly lie down inside in winter, when their thick woolly coats give plenty of protection. Oat straw is best avoided, as it is rather sweet tasting and so a pony may eat a considerable quantity of it. This does no serious harm. But, the straw is bulky and has relatively little nutritional value so the pony is filled up to no good purpose and has nothing to lie on when all the bedding is eaten!

Wood shavings make a good bed for a pony, and are particularly useful for those few greedy animals which will eat any type of straw bedding. Odd blocks of wood should be picked out of the shavings. The same applies to sawdust which can be used instead. It is not as good a material as shavings as it tends to heat up as soon as it gets soiled and a little damp. This damages the animal's feet. Particular care has therefore to be taken to keep sawdust clean and dry, and consequently an ample supply is necessary. It is generally economical in terms of cost, like wood shavings, being available free from many timber yards.

Peat moss is sometimes used and is very good for the purpose. It is very absorbent so that there is little smell when it is soiled. This does not mean that cleaning out can be neglected. Like any other dirty bedding, peat will rot down in the stable and the pony's feet will suffer. The peat moss itself should be mainly close-fibred and, if it is of good quality, will contain little earth or stony material. It has the snag that it tends to be rather expensive in some areas.

Shredded paper can also be used as bedding but is expensive. Like shavings, sawdust, and peat, it is useful when eating bedding is a problem. When bedded-up 'fresh', all these materials are good for ponies which are allergic to moulds in straw. In deep litter they have no advantage. Dead leaves and bracken ferns may save money, but make unsatisfactory bedding as they quickly become saturated with urine. Bracken can cause severe illness if large amounts are eaten. Sand is also unsuitable as it is cold, and causes colic if eaten.

Keeping the Stable Clean
A pony is quite a large animal and its diet (hay and grass) contains a considerable amount of material which it is unable to digest. Consequently large quantities of manure and urine are produced, which soil the bedding. The dung and the wet bedding should be removed daily – 'mucked out' – and the bedding made up again with fresh. This is probably preferable to the 'deep litter' system, where soiled bedding is allowed to build up gradually and a thick layer of new straw is added to the top to provide a warm bed for

the pony. This deep litter has one advantage in that it requires less attention each day, though in other respects it is less satisfactory.

The daily 'mucking out' of the stable is an unpleasant task, not least because of the strong smell which impregnates the clothes and footwear of the operator. If you would rather everyone did not know just what you have been doing, an overall and gumboots are advised. The unsoiled straw is first sorted with a pitchfork and stacked in a dry corner of the box. Dirty bedding and dung are loaded into a wheelbarrow (or onto a piece of sacking) to be carted away; for this purpose a four-pronged dungfork and a shovel are useful. The floor of the stable is finally swept clean with a stiff yardbroom. It may be necessary to throw a bucket of water over the floor to complete the cleaning process. This will also flush out drains, which tend to get blocked very easily with fragments of straw or other bedding.

The bedding is best left loosely stacked in one corner of the stable for some hours, to give it a chance to dry, and to allow the floor to dry and air. During this time the windows and door should be left open. This is only likely to be possible if the pony is turned out for the day or night; otherwise it may be necessary to put the bedding down again at once, whether the floor is wet or not.

Disposal of Manure

Horse manure, particularly that from straw bedding, is an excellent garden fertilizer which helps to compensate for the cost of the straw. To be of use in the garden, the manure needs to be well rotted. During the rotting process a manure heap will shrink, helping to reduce the volume of material to be disposed of. The way the heap is stacked influences the rotting process.

The manure should be stacked in a heap which has a flat top and vertical sides, the material being spread evenly on the top and levelled off. The purpose of this is to ensure that rain water soaks into the heap, rather than running off as it would off a haycock-shaped mound, as the water is essential to the rotting process. This is also improved by the addition of potassium nitrate or some other composting agent. This type of vertical sided stack also looks neater than an untidy, sprawling heap. To help keep the manure heap square or rectangular a two- or three-sided frame can be constructed of vertical sheets of corrugated iron nailed to posts

Fig. 13. Horse manure is a very useful garden fertilizer when it is allowed to rot down in a proper stack.

two or three feet high. A smarter alternative can be built from concrete blocks.

The manure stack is best placed at some distance from the stable itself, so that none of its odour is noticeable in the building. A hard path of concrete, bricks or – at least – a series of wooden planks, is usually necessary if the daily wheeling of a full barrow of manure is not to make the track unpleasantly muddy in winter.

Making the Pony's Bed
To lay the clean straw into a comfortable bed for a pony is not simply a matter of kicking the bedding over the floor. This will result in its being scattered in lumps; thickly here and thinly there. The bedding should be shaken down with a fork so that it makes a level surface with some extra banking up against the walls of the stable. The purpose of this is to prevent draughts blowing round the pony's legs and to avoid the animal becoming trapped or 'cast' between the wall and a mound of bedding in the middle of the stable when he lies down.

To make a new 'bed' for a stable 10 foot square (at least 3

metres by 3 metres), about 50–70 lb (23–32kg) of straw are required (most bales are about 56 lb/25kg). The amount varies considerably depending on the quality and type of bedding used and the size of the pony. To reduce the amount of straw put down initially is in fact a false economy. This seems to increase rather than decrease the amount of bedding which has to be thrown out because it is soiled, as well as increasing the risk of self-injury to the pony.

Generally between 10-20 lb (4.5-9kg) of new bedding have to be added daily to replace dirty material. Less is required if the pony is out for some of the time. The new straw is usually added at night, and it requires careful shaking out to disentangle the 'folds' of the bale. The bale string (or wire) should be taken off carefully and removed from the stable to prevent the pony eating it, or getting tangled in it. Ideally shaking up new straw should be done when the pony is not in the stable. It takes twenty minutes for the dust and mould spores to settle down again afterwards.

If a pony is kept in the stable for a majority of the time it may be necessary to 'skip out' or remove the heaps of dung once or twice a day, besides mucking out each morning. The 'skipping out' helps to keep the stable clean and sweet-smelling and prevents the manure being trampled into the bedding. The dung is removed with a fork and placed in a 'skip' which is emptied onto the manure heap. The 'skip' was traditionally a wicker or rush basket. Today the purpose is served just as well by a metal or plastic container which is kept hanging with the other stable cleaning implements. These can be kept on nails driven into the wall, and should include a yard broom, four-pronged dungfork, and shovel; a wire rake is also useful for clearing areas which are not hard-surfaced.

'Deep Litter'

As an alternative to the thorough daily mucking-out of the stable, a 'deep litter' system may be adopted. This involves only the removal of droppings each day, the wet straw being allowed to build up beneath a thick layer of dry. It is sometimes thought that the use of 'deep litter' saves bedding material. This is not so, as enough fresh litter has to be added each day to ensure that the animal has a dry surface to lie on. Time spent on the pony each day

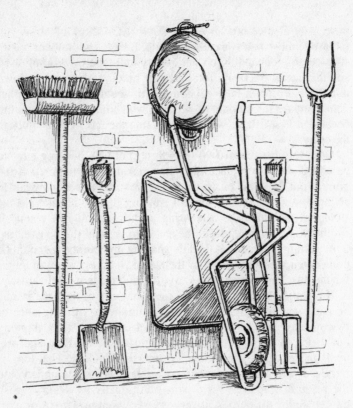

Fig. 14. Stable cleaning equipment: yard broom, shovel, 'skip' (plastic bowl with handles), wheelbarrow, 4-pronged dungfork and pitchfork. The tools are hung on nails driven into the wall.

is saved, however. There is the advantage that whoever looks after the pony does not have clothes and hair impregnated with the scent of the animal. This is a help if you are trying to persuade someone else to care for the pony while you are away. The litter does have to be cleaned out completely every few months. This is a large and not particularly pleasant task.

The deep litter may have the advantage, from the pony's point of view, that it provides a warmer bed than a sparsely-littered, daily-cleaned stable. The deep litter itself may produce a little warmth. From the owner's point of view the warm, moist, rotting litter may damage the stable walls with continuous contact, particularly if these are of wood. Some bedding materials are also unsuitable for deep litter; among them are sawdust and peat moss.

Ponies which Eat Their Bedding
Most ponies will pick over fresh straw bedding and consume any odd tasty stalks they find in it. This does no harm provided they do not eat too much straw. Some animals will, however, eat straw in large quantities – so much that it becomes injurious – 'a vice.'

There are a number of reasons for this tendency. One is straight-forward hunger. The pony is simply not getting enough other food. The remedy here is obvious. These ponies are often in poor physical condition because not enough attention is paid to the quantity and quality of hay that is being fed.

Fig. 15. Most ponies pick over fresh bedding.

Another reason is the quite common one of greed; an already tubby pony gobbling up anything that is possibly edible. To prevent this the pony may be bedded on peat moss, wood shavings or sawdust; if straw has to be used, it may be sprinkled with a strong-smelling disinfectant. Mixing the fresh straw with that remaining from the previous day also helps to deter the stuffpot.

Occasionally a pony may develop a depraved appetite, consuming bedding of any sort, and maybe even its own dung. Such quirks are sometimes due to heavy infestation with worms, particularly in the young animal, or to mineral deficiency. Both are matters about which you should consult your veterinary surgeon.

Boredom may make a pony eat the bedding for amusement. Confined alone for 23 hours out of 24 with nothing to eat but the daily hay and concentrate ration, is it really surprising? Any animal benefits from having a stable with a view into a yard or area where people and animals are coming and going. Company of another pony, donkey, sheep or cow also helps the bored animal, as does being turned out for a few hours a day. As with all so-called 'vices' it is better to spend a few minutes trying to work out *why* the pony eats the bedding. This is preferable to spending time and effort trying to prevent the vice by putting on a muzzle or tying the pony up for hours on end or changing to less palatable bedding.

6

EQUIPPING THE STABLE

Now you have got a suitable building for the pony, equipped with a door and window to permit access and ventilation plus a warm dry bed for the animal to lie on. The next considerations are the stable fittings and utensils. These include such items as water buckets, feed tins and hay nets; the essentials which contain the pony's day to day necessities.

Water Container
The type of trough most suitable for the field has already been described and would be far too big to use in the stable. Indoors, the pony's water can be provided in a bucket, which has the great advantage that it is easy to clean. *To thrive, a pony must have a constant supply of fresh water.* The water bucket should be checked and topped up if necessary at least three times a day, though you should automatically check the water supply every time you go into the stable. Every morning, if the pony is in, the water bucket should be emptied, rinsed out, and re-filled, as animals seem to dislike water which has stood around overnight. It is best to remove the water bucket from the stable while the box is being mucked out, so that small pieces of soiled material do not get into it. These, understandably, make the water undrinkable.

Scrubbing out the water bucket and rinsing it out thoroughly once a week also helps to ensure that the water is palatable. If this is not done a slight slime sometimes develops on the inside of the bucket. This appears irrespective of the material from which the bucket is made. In this regard there is little to choose between galvanised iron, rubber and heavy plastic. Whatever it is made of, the bucket needs to be solid so that it will not be split by a casual knock from a hoof. It should have a capacity of at least two gallons. If this is too heavy for you to carry when full, you may find it easier to make several journeys with a smaller bucket to fill it up.

The pony's water bucket is generally stood in a corner of the loose box, normally by the door and preferably where it will not get full of hay, nor where the pony is likely to foul it. Some ponies, fortunately not many, develop the naughty trick of playing football with the water bucket, soaking the bedding and breaking the bucket. For these animals a loop attached to the wall, into which the bucket fits, may be the answer.

An automatic water drinker connected to the mains supply is the ideal way to ensure the pony has access to water at all times – thus avoiding any problems that might occur as a result of water deprivation. Disadvantages are: they are hard to clean, can freeze in cold weather and may become jammed with hay or bedding, so they must be checked twice daily to ensure they are functioning properly.

Mangers

Very important to any pony is the container in which the meals are given, in particular the pony nuts or grain. There has long been argument as to whether it is better for ponies to eat from ground level as they would naturally, or from a raised manger which cannot be kicked over. In practice, it seems that the height from which a pony feeds is of little importance provided it is not below floor level, or higher than about 30 inches (75cm) above the ground.

Feeding at floor level is certainly simplest as the pony is given his meal in a bucket or bowl which is removed when he has finished. These containers have the advantage of being easy to rinse out and keep clean. If you feed the pony from a bucket do remember two things. First, that there should be no sharp projections from the attachments of the bucket's handle, on which the pony might injure himself or catch his headcollar. Second, that the base of the bucket should be wide enough to allow the pony's nose to the bottom in comfort. Otherwise it can be very distressing if the animal cannot reach all the food.

A shallower, larger feed bowl is really preferable to a bucket as it enables an animal to get at the feed more easily and see what it is. It is also harder to tip up. A good quality plastic washing up bowl makes an excellent feed container and is unlikely to be very expensive. Alternatively, a galvanised iron bowl, with vertical sides, is available and is suitable for a pony's food or water.

Some ponies persistently paw the ground as they eat and often knock over their feed bowl so that food is wasted. For such, a manger attached to the wall is most useful. It is possible to buy triangular plastic or galvanised iron mangers which can be fixed neatly into the corner of the stable. One of these may be more economical than buying a continual stream of new plastic bowls to replace ones which have been trampled on and broken. Such mangers are easy to clean and, like any other container, need an occasional scrub.

Salt Licks

Most ponies appreciate a lump of salt which they can lick while they stand in the stable or shelter. The salt can be provided in the field but, being soluble, it is washed away by rain, so is better kept indoors. The salt can be provided as a rectangular block which slides into a special metal holder screwed to the wall. The most suitable height for this depends on the size of the pony, but usually between 3 and 3½ feet (about 1 metre) above the ground is comfortable. Alternatively, a lump of rock salt may be kept in

Fig. 16. A pony appreciates a salt lick.

the manger for the pony to lick.

This supply of extra salt is not essential to the animal's survival but most ponies have a natural craving for salt, which they may satisfy by eating earth if no salt is available. The two elements of salt, sodium and chlorine, are vital to all living things. The pony's normal daily requirement is supplied in his food, but very hard work, which causes sweating and consequent loss of salt, means that extra may be needed. With a salt lick, the pony can take what is required.

Feeding Hay

In old stables a hay rack was always provided. This was usually fixed to the wall some feet from the ground, the horse pulling down the hay as it was wanted. This type reduced wastage but had one disadvantage. As the hay was pulled down, small particles of dry grass and dust were scattered in the animal's eyes and nostrils. It is, therefore, now considered wrong to feed hay from a container above the horse's head.

The natural way of feeding is to give the pony hay in a heap on the ground. Unfortunately, this leads to wastage as the animal tends to pick over the hay, eating the most delicious stalks first and trampling on the rest. The wastage can be avoided by giving the hay in an open-topped rack 2 or 3 feet (just under 1 metre) above the ground so that the less tasty bits simply fall to the bottom and are not trampled. Such a rack is, however, expensive, and requires proper fitting. It also takes up considerable space even when empty. In a loose box this is more of a disadvantage than in a stall, where it is common for a manger, hay rack and holder for a water bucket to be combined in one fitting along the front wall.

A justifiably popular method of feeding hay to ponies is in hay-nets. Made of thick, preferably tarred, string, or nylon, the net is stuffed with hay and then tied to a ring in the wall of the stable or, outside, to a strong fence. It should be secured as shown in fig. 17 with the end of the cord tied to the bottom of the net. This stops the net sagging as the hay is eaten, preventing the pony pawing the empty net and getting its feet caught up in it.

Storing the Pony's Food

Hay and 'concentrates' – usually oats or pony nuts – are expensive and therefore deserve proper storage. There is also the serious risk that any type of food which has been badly kept, and allowed to become damp and mouldy, may give the pony colic.

Hay should be stored in a dry building out of reach of the pony. The building may be open sided and should be well-ventilated, with the hay stacked so as to allow plenty of air to circulate. If you have reason to believe that the floor of the building is the slightest bit damp – and the floors of most out-buildings are – then it is an economy to make the bottom layer of bales of straw. These are cheaper than hay and thus represent less of a loss if they have to be discarded for mouldiness.

Straw or other bedding is bulky, and is usually stacked alongside the hay. If you have enough storage space it is often most economical and least bother to buy a whole winter's supply of hay and straw in the autumn. Use a reputable supplier who, though he may charge a little more, is unlikely to supply bad material as he has his reputation to consider.

The hay store should always be kept neat and tidy. Use up the hay and straw bale by bale so that you do not have several half-

How to hang a hay-net . . .

. . . so that it does not dangle on the ground when it is empty.
Fig. 17.

used bales loose on the floor getting dirty. Most bales are tied with string or wire. Your penknife, scissors or wire cutters are less likely to get lost if they are fitted with a loop of string so that they can be kept hung up. When you first open a new bale, pick out the string or wire and hang it safely out of the way, on a hook put up specially for this purpose. A useful addition to the hay store is a spring balance, big enough to weigh up to about 20 lb (9kg). This will enable you to check just how much your pony is eating.

'Concentrate' feeds are usually supplied in paper or plastic bags, but, paper bags are not damp-proof nor are they a sufficient barrier to rats or mice. So, some kind of dry vermin-proof container is needed to store concentrates. Proper corn bins can be expensive but a metal or plastic dustbin (preferably a new one) or a redundant chest freezer make satisfactory alternatives. A clever pony can knock off a dustbin lid to get at food but the animal should never have access to the feed store anyway. Remember that ponies have died as a result of gorging themselves on concentrates.

The feed store is a good place to keep feed bowls and water buckets. You should also have one or more scoops. These are small bowls (e.g. saucepans) which hold a known amount of each type of food and can be used to measure a set amount into a pony's bowl. This helps to ensure that the pony gets its correct ration. A scoop holding one pound of oats (volume of about one and a half pints) is suitable.

Tying Up the Pony

A tethering ring in the stable is useful not only for hanging up the hay-net, but for tying up the pony as well. When you are grooming, for example, or looking at the shoes, it is essential that the pony is tethered securely. The tethering ring itself consists of a metal ring attached to the wall about 4 feet (just over 1 metre) from the ground. When tied up, the pony's lead rope should be tied to a small loop of bale cord attached to the ring. This cord will break and release the pony should it become frightened and panic for some reason, thereby reducing the risk of injury.

Headcollars and halters are also essential stable equipment. A headcollar is a harness of leather or nylon strapping which fits the pony's head. It does not have a bit and can be worn when the pony is loose in the field. With a rope attached to the back D-ring the headcollar is used for leading and tying up the pony. It should fit comfortably, so that the noseband does not interfere with the jaws as the pony chews, though it should not be so large that it flaps freely or slips off.

A leather headcollar is an expensive item; one of nylon is not usually so costly. More economical still is a halter, which is a simple harness of rope and rope strapping. The leading rope is an integral part of it (see fig. 18). It is made up and slipped over the pony's head. A knot is tied to secure the leading rope at the left side of the noseband, to prevent it being pulled uncomfortably tight.

Either a headcollar and rope or a halter can be used for leading and tying up a pony and it is essential to have one or the other. The rope halter gives you less control over the animal, and the pony cannot be turned loose in the field in it. A proper headcollar, from which you have only to remove the leading rope when you turn the pony out, is therefore preferable.

When tied up, a pony should have sufficient rope to allow for

A headcollar and rope . . .

, , , or a halter

Fig. 18.

movement of the head, but not enough to allow the forelegs to become entangled. The knot used for tying up animals should always be of the quick-release type – a half-hitch with a loop through it (see fig 19 opposite) – so that a jerk on the free end releases the animal. This is most important as all ponies are inclined to panic if anything goes wrong. By pulling back hard on the headrope the knot by which the animal is tied (if not of the quick-release type) can be drawn so tight that it is impossible to undo. Sometimes there is a problem with the cunning pony which has learnt to undo a quick-release knot by pulling the free end with the teeth. This may be discouraged if you pass the free end back through the loop again; it means that the knot takes a moment longer to untie in an emergency, but it still will not pull up tight.

In a loose box a pony is unlikely to be tied up for long periods and is generally tied directly to the tethering ring. In a stall, however, there is a problem. The animal requires enough rope to lie down comfortably, but with this length dangling from the head, the pony is likely to get caught up at other times. The problem is solved by passing the headrope through a loop on the manger and then through a wooden ball, to which it is secured with – of course – a quick release knot. This method allows the spare rope to be taken up, but it is played out again as the pony lies down. The length of rope is usually enough to allow the animal to stand normally when the wooden ball is resting on the ground.

And Outside . . .
Outside the stable there are a number of fittings which make life easier. A hook by the stable door, for example, provides somewhere to keep the pony's headcollar. Then there can be no excuse for just dumping it on the ground when the pony is in the stable, or for leading the animal about by the mane because the halter isn't handy. Hooks are also necessary to fasten back doors and windows so that they do not bang about in the wind.

A water tap near the stable door is convenient, reducing the distance over which the water has to be carried and making it possible to hose down the flooring. All stable work is made easier if the building has a small hard standing outside. In winter you do not want to plunge into a sea of mud every time you go in and out.

If the stable is not already in a field, a fence round the area will prevent the pony's going too far should he get free. This is particularly important near a road.

Fire!
Fire in a stable is a scene of horror. It is all too easy to lull oneself

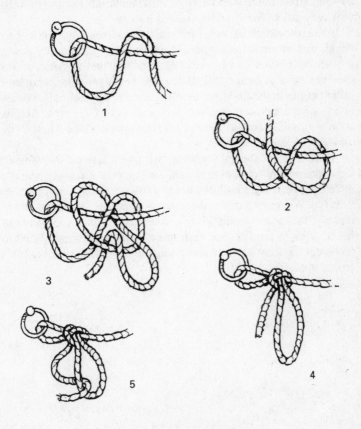

Fig. 19. Tying a pony up.
Steps 1–4 show how to tie a quick-release knot. To release the knot, pull the free end.
For ponies which learn to undo the knot themselves, the free end is pulled through the loop as in no. 5.

into a sense of false security, that 'it could never happen to us'; unfortunately fire can, and does, break out anywhere.

Some buildings are in particular danger from fire. Thatched roofs or timber stables where unfire-proofed roofing felt has been used are at special risk. Many fires start as sparks from faulty electrical wiring. Whatever they are made of, all stables have dry hay and straw in them and both of these materials burn very well, so a very strict 'No Smoking' rule is a must.

If fire should break out, the first thing to remember is not to panic: that never helps anyone. If the fire is small, rapidly douse it with cold water – a bucket full is better than nothing, and a pressure hose is better still. If the fire is bigger, first warn any other people in the building and then remove any animals. Ponies and dogs are best tethered securely well out of the way. And as soon as possible contact the fire brigade by telephone. (In the UK dial 999 for emergency.)

A fire extinguisher of the water jet type is a good investment, kept somewhere obvious and easily accessible. It could make the difference between a building being destroyed or saved. However, this type of extinguisher does have quite an important snag; namely, that some young pony-owners may find it too heavy to lift or point at the fire. For their use a hose permanently fitted to the water tap may be much more satisfactory, as long as it doesn't freeze up.

7

GRASS AS PONY FOOD

The best feed for a pony is grass. Not only is it the natural food, but grazing also provides the animal with continuous occupation and exercise. But even though grazing may be the pony's natural way of life, simply being turned loose in a paddock and left to fend for itself is not the way to keep the animal in first-class condition throughout the year.

One important reason for this is that grass grows well only when there is sufficient moisture, warmth and sunlight. Its nutritive value therefore varies greatly from season to season. A wild pony could probably scratch up enough to keep going during the hard times of winter and early spring because of the vast tracts of moorland and hill over which to roam with no work to do. The domesticated animal is in a different position, and, enclosed in a small field, has less opportunity to search for edible material when grass is short. Through the winter months, from about November to May, your pony requires extra food in the form of hay and perhaps 'concentrates' – grain and horse nuts.

In the early summer the situation is reversed. The winter shortage of grass is replaced by plenty, and quite often excess. In May particularly the grass is highly nutritious and ponies which have free access to it tend to become over-fat and sleepy and may also suffer diseases of obesity such as laminitis, so-called 'fever in the feet'. At this time of year the pony may have to be shut away from the grass for part of each day to ensure protection from the ill-effects of greed.

The Grazing Pony's Day
A pony living out at grass tends to settle into a fixed routine which is seldom broken, unless disturbed by humans. The animal will probably graze for between sixteen and eighteen hours out of the

twenty-four, though this depends to some extent on the quality of the herbage. Later in the summer, though the bulk of grass is still large, its feeding value drops and the pony's intake has to increase to compensate. On an average day a middle-sized pony will eat 50–75 lb (23–34kg) of grass.

The most serious eating is done in the few hours just after dawn, and in the period before dusk, when the dew is on the grass. A pony seldom does much grazing while it is actually dark. In winter when the days are short, grazing time is reduced – another reason why supplementary feeding is so important at this time. In the early morning the pony grazes hard for a couple of hours and will then have a short rest, perhaps a drink at the water trough, and may lie down for a little while and doze. Later in the day quite a bit of time may be spent in what could be called 'casual grazing', moving about the field at random and picking, rather than eating continuously.

This tendency to 'pick' helps to account for the reputation horses have as bad grazers. They are inclined to eat all the most tasty grasses, leaving the ones they do not like to grow tall and rank. Cattle graze much more evenly: having no top teeth they have to tear out the grass in bunches instead of biting it neatly as

Key to fig. 20.
Desirable pasture grasses.
1. Timothy grass (*phleum pratense*): may take a couple of years to establish, but very palatable, grows well, and comes up early in Spring.
2. Perennial rye grass (*Lolium perenne*): a very valuable grass.
3. Meadow fescue (*Festucata pratensis*): Slow to establish, but very palatable.
4. White clover (*Trifolium repens*): Tasty, digestible and drought-resistant. Clover also helps other grasses in the 'sward' by nitrogen fixation.
5. Red clover (*Trifolium pratense*): Drought-resistant and palatable.
Common, but not such good pasture grasses.
6. Cocksfoot (*Dactylis glomerata*): a tough plant but not very palatable, and not of high feeding value.
7. Rough-stalked meadow grass (*Poa trivialis*): Tends to grow for only a small part of the year, but smothers more productive grasses.
8. Yorkshire fog (*Holcus lauatus*): a tough grass, but of little value as food.
9. Tall fescue (*Festuca arundinalea*): a native of road verges, not palatable but grows from early Spring until late Autumn.
Weeds no-one wants.
10. Stinging Nettles.   **11.** Thistles.   **12.** Docks.
All best removed by regular cutting, and/or spraying with weedkiller.

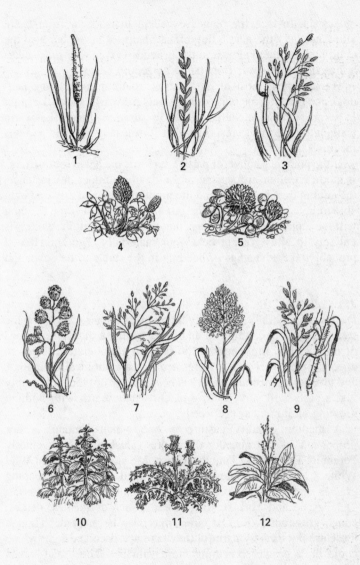

Fig. 20. Grasses and weeds (key on facing page).

horses do. In fact, the pony's excellent incisors, or front teeth, allow not only the neat biting off of blades of grass, but also the ability to bite them almost to the ground. This is why grass takes a long time to recover from being grazed by horses.

Having spent most of the daytime roaming around the paddock and grazing, the pony usually settles down to spend the night in some suitable sheltered place. In summer it may be warm enough to lie down to rest. In winter it is usually too cold and wet for this.

If the pony is stabled for part of the time, the behaviour pattern is modified. Shut in for most of the day in summer, for instance, the animal may have to spend the night grazing and rely on being able to lie down and rest in the box by day, so that some bedding will be appreciated. Stabling the pony at night in winter is unlikely to alter grazing behaviour materially. The animal will probably take advantage of bedding in the stable to lie down and rest.

The Paddock

Ponies are generally good at living on fairly meagre rations by the standards of, for example, a dairy cow giving a thousand gallons of milk a year. Most equines do best on a moderate, though an adequate diet. Very rich pastures and leys are not ideal for a pony, and grazing of medium quality is best. This is not meant to imply that a pony will survive on a patch of bare earth with nothing growing on it but a sea of weeds.

A medium quality pasture is one which contains a fair proportion of the nutritionally more valuable grasses, chiefly Perennial Rye Grass, Timothy Grass, Meadow Fescue and Wild White Clover. With these will be mixed less useful feeding grasses, such as Wild Cocksfoot, Rough-stalked Meadow grasses, Tall Fescue and Yorkhire Fog. Weeds, such as thistles, nettles, couch grass and Wild Oat Grass may also be present. Though these are not directly harmful they take up space and light which could have grown something more valuable. The broad-leaved weeds, such as nettles and thistles, can be controlled by spraying with weedkiller (when the pony is being kept elsewhere) or by cutting the weeds before they seed. If the weed problem gets really out of hand there may be nothing for it but to get the paddock ploughed and re-sown with a good grass mixture.

Poisonous weeds are more of a problem and it is worth keeping a watch on what is growing in the paddock. Some apparently harmless trees and plants can be an unexpected problem. Oak trees, for example, can shed large numbers of acorns after an autumn gale. Eaten by a hungry or greedy pony, the acorns can cause serious, sometimes fatal, illness.

The Yew is a very poisonous tree and causes a large proportion of the cases of poisoning of herbivora. Particularly after a storm there is a risk that branches will have blown down and wilted and at this time the animals seem more ready to eat them. If there is a Yew tree in the field the safest course is to fence it off completely so that no sprigs or twigs from it can fall within reach of a pony, or any other livestock.

Some poisonous plants are best removed by 'routing', that is, simply pulling them up, roots and all, and taking them right away to the bonfire. Ragwort is one of these; a fairly tall plant with deep golden flowers it is an unpleasantly common sight in fields where ponies are grazed. It is a very poisonous plant but takes effect slowly. The liver of the pony that eats it suffers progressive damage. Because removal of this plant from the field is not a difficult task, nor is it an unpleasant one on a sunny day, it seems silly to expose your pony to the danger of Ragwort poisoning.

The incidence of Ragwort poisoning seems to vary from year to year, and this is probably related to the palatability of the Ragwort as it grows in the spring. In some years it appears that horses are not put off eating Ragwort, whilst in others they will invariably leave it to grow to its full height without touching it. One of the most dangerous periods is when the Ragwort has been cut, if it is left in the field. Once the Ragwort is wilted and turning into hay, it becomes fairly palatable to horses who will happily eat it. The advice to pull the Ragwort out by its roots, and remove it to a bonfire, is therefore very necessary. Care should also be taken that if hay is to be cut, Ragwort plants are not included in the cut crop. As the hay is wilted and baled, again the Ragwort will become palatable and is just as poisonous when eaten in the middle of winter as when eaten in full flower.

The plants of the Hemlock family, including Water Dropwort and Cowbane, are also extremely poisonous. Unlike Ragwort,

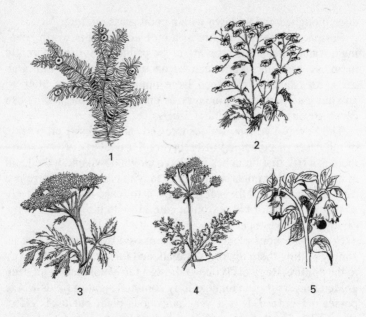

Fig. 21. Dangerous trees and plants.
Yew trees (1) should be fenced off, or the lower boughs removed. Ragwort (2) can be removed by 'routing'. Members of the Hemlock family, Cowbane (3) and Water Dropwort (4), are very poisonous, as is Deadly Nightshade (5).

which usually grows in sunny parts of the field, these succulent plants prefer damp hedgerows and ditches. So does Deadly Nightshade, also very poisonous. These, too, can be pulled up and removed quite easily, though one should be careful to wash the hands afterwards.

The prompt removal of these uprooted weeds is very important for most poisonous plants seem to become more attractive to animals as they wilt. This is true of many other greenstuffs too. Privet hedge trimmings, for instance, are sometimes eaten greedily and with unfortunate results by a pony who would do no more than nibble at a shoot of the hedge itself. Besides their increased palatability if they are allowed to wilt, poisonous plants may occasionally attract a very hungry animal or one with an appetite depraved as a result of excessive worm infestation or because of mineral deficiency.

'Horse-sick Pasture'

The bad effect of ponies on grassland has already been mentioned. The tendency of these animals to bite some areas bare, yet leave others to grow rank and coarse, may suggest to the owners of ponies – wrongly – that while there is long grass on the field there is plenty for a pony to eat. But the animal would much sooner go hungry than eat this long herbage.

Another reason for these patchy grazing habits is that ponies tend to deposit droppings only in certain areas, and naturally, will not graze round their own dung. Fortunately, cows have no such

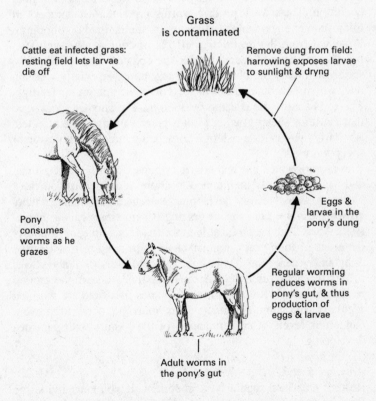

Grass
is contaminated

Cattle eat infected grass:
resting field lets larvae
die off

Remove dung from field:
harrowing exposes larvae
to sunlight & dryng

Pony
consumes
worms as he
grazes

Eggs &
larvae in the
pony's dung

Regular worming
reduces worms in
pony's gut, & thus
production of
eggs & larvae

Adult worms in
the pony's gut

Fig. 22. Life-cycle of the pony's worm-parasites. The breaks in the line show the ways in which this cycle can be broken.

dislike and will level the grass in a field very well; alternatively, patches of very long grass can be cut with a mowing machine to encourage new growth. The ideal solution, if time permits, is to pick up the droppings with a shovel or pair of boards and remove them in a wheelbarrow.

In some respects the strong tendency of a pony to avoid droppings when grazing is an advantage, as it may help to reduce the numbers of worm parasites which are acquired. These are small worms which inhabit the pony's gut, where they live on the food passing through. Their presence reduces the benefit that the animal derives from food and they may lead to weakness and poor condition. These very prolific worms produce vast numbers of microscopic eggs which pass out in the animal's droppings. Protected from the destructive effects of cold weather and sunlight by the heap of faecal matter, the eggs develop quickly to a state where they are able to infect any pony, especially a young one, which consumes them in the course of grazing or feeding. The eggs simply die if eaten by an animal of another species, so that cattle or sheep grazing with a pony would not be affected. Similarly there is little risk of a pony being infected with cattle or sheep worms.

A pasture which has had horses or ponies on it for a long time, and has been poorly maintained, becomes a dangerous source of worm eggs, as well as developing the characteristically patchy growth of grass. This sort of grazing is sometimes called 'horsesick'. Apart from keeping cattle in the field for a time, or 'topping' the areas of long grass, regular chain harrowing to disperse the dung and expose parasites to light and cold is also valuable. So is rolling the field, often done at the same time, to keep the ground reasonably level. It is vital that all ponies in a field are wormed regularly and simultaneously. This must be done to prevent dangerous levels of contamination of the pasture with parasites developing.

Area per Pony

Resting grassland regularly is important. If you can, divide the field into two halves and let the animals graze them alternately, rather than letting them run over the whole area all the time. The grass in each half is given a chance to recover and while it is empty a large portion of parasites on the grass will also succumb, thus reducing that problem, too.

If the pasture is of middling quality, not too lush but not over-sparse either, then one pony should be able to live off one and a half to two acres, plus some extra food in winter. The quality of the grass, the way it is managed, how much fertilizer is spread on it, and so on, all have a bearing on what proportion of the pony's food comes from the field.

The best pointer to the quality of the grass is the condition of the animal. Ponies that are sleek, alert and reasonably plump are probably getting enough to eat. If yours stands miserably with the coat staring and the body thin and 'tucked up', then it is time you increased the rations. The season of the year affects the amount of grass that grows. Is the winter unusually hard, or unexpectedly mild? Is the spring abnormally late? These factors alter the condition of a pony living on grass, so that supplementary feeding has to be modified accordingly.

In the early summer there may be too much grass on a paddock and even as small a field as one of one and three-quarter acres will probably provide enough food to make a pony overfat. During this period it is usually necessary to restrict the food intake. This can be done either by shutting the pony in a stable for the daytime – where it will have the added advantage of being away from the pestering flies – or by running other ponies or cattle on the field to help eat down the grass.

Alternatively, part of the field can be fenced off with an electric fence. One part may be used to make some hay of your own on which to feed the pony during the winter. However, making good hay is not all that easy and there is a risk that you might produce only a mouldy, damp material which could be worse for the pony than nothing at all. If you decide to try to get some hay off the paddock, it is worth asking a local farmer or agricultural contractor to do the hard work for you. He probably would be willing to advise you on the care of the pasture, too.

Catching the Pony

Most ponies seem to enjoy being free in a grassy paddock; most are also good and reliably easy to catch. A pony is far easier to catch if it was left already wearing a headcollar. Then all you have

Fig. 23. 'The pony is concentrating on the food that you are bringing . . . '

to do is to carry the leading rope in your pocket or behind your back and walk up to the animal. Talking as you approach helps. Develop the habit of always taking a tit-bit – a crust of bread or a piece of carrot – when you go into the field, whether you intend catching the pony or not. This gets the idea ingrained that you always bring something edible. The pony is then concentrating on the food you are bringing and thoughts do not turn to running away. Walk up, give the tit-bit, gently pat the neck and quietly hook the rope onto the headstall, ready to lead the pony to the gate.

Unfortunately, things do not always work out as smoothly as this and the pony may decide to play hard to get. This is more likely if you approach noisily or hurriedly, or if the pony is not expecting a bribe in the form of a tit-bit or a handful of oats in the bottom of a bucket. Ponies which are difficult to catch anyway are always more so if they are not turned out with a headcollar on. They seem to revert to the wild state when they are wearing no man-made harness.

There are few things more irritating than a pony which tries to avoid being caught, particularly if you have been looking forward to a lovely ride on a glorious summer morning and even more so if you had intended going to a gymkhana or Pony Club rally. (The possibility that you may not be able to catch the animal on the morning is one good reason for shutting a pony in overnight before such occasions.) The best immediate solution to the problems is probably to leave the pony for half an hour, and then return with a feed in a bucket. Few ponies can resist the prospect of a delicious meal. It is important that you do not allow yourself to become impatient, as the animal will sense this very quickly and it will only make things worse.

In the long run, visiting the pony frequently in the field, always taking with you a tit-bit, will get your pony into the habit of looking to see what you have brought. For a really bad uncatchable, give a small feed at the same time each day – whether you intend to go for a ride or not. This will get the pony into the habit of coming to the gate to meet you, and used to being stroked and petted. It is a good policy to catch up the pony daily anyway so that you can look the animal over for injuries or illness. It also gives you an opportunity to check the level in the water trough while you are in the field.

Hay, Cut Grass and Silage
Hay is grass which is cut and allowed to dry in the sun during the early part of the summer. At this time the weather is, hopefully, hot and dry. The grass itself is of high nutritive value as it comes into flower. The quality of hay depends on two factors, the type of grass from which it is made and the timing, with regard to the weather, of the 'making' process. This also includes correct stacking.

Hay is divided into various categories depending on the type of grassland from which it came. 'Seeds Hay' is rather coarse and is made from a specially seeded mixture, usually of a Rye-grass and clover. It may be cut at a late stage of growth and be rather stemmy. 'Meadow Hay' on the other hand, tends to be softer and is made by cutting a meadow which is a permanent pasture. It usually contains a wider variety of grasses (and some weeds) than does 'seeds hay' and is often greener with a higher proportion of leaf to stem.

This is not necessarily a bad thing provided the hay has been well 'made', which means that it has not been rained on while lying out in the field. Good hay is sweet-smelling with no trace of mould or mustiness and is slightly greenish in colour. The quality of the hay determines its value – or worthlessness – as a feed for your pony. To buy poor hay is an entirely false economy as you will have to give far more of it, as well as subjecting the animal to various health risks (especially COPD). Recently-made hay should not be fed to horses as it can cause serious digestive problems. Ideally, hay should be stacked for six months before use. In the autumn, hay made the previous summer should be used if possible. When new hay is first fed it should be introduced gradually, i.e. mixed with old hay for a few days.

The amount of hay has to vary inversely with the amount and quality of the grazing a pony is getting, and according to the animal's condition. (Does the pony seem well?) It depends too, but to a lesser degree, on the amount of work which is done and the amount of other 'concentrate' feed you are giving. Hay is really a pony's staple food in winter, in the same way that grass is in summer, and should not be reduced whatever the state of finances. It also has the great advantage, particularly for young riders, that ponies can consume and enjoy large quantities of good quality hay without getting above themselves or becoming naughty.

As a rough guide, during the winter a pony of about 12.2 HH requires 5–9 lb (2.3–4kg) of good hay daily, a 13.2 HH pony 6–11 lb (2.7–5kg) and a 14.2 HH pony 8–12 lb (3.5–5.5kg) daily. This does, however, assume that there is also access to good pasture. If the pony is stabled, or on very poor pasture, or the ground is covered with snow and frost, the hay requirement would be about doubled, and the animal would need a 'concentrate' feed as well. It is necessary to feed hay from about mid-October until the middle or end of April. It is never worth delaying the start of hay-feeding in the interest of economy as this means that the pony begins the cold weather rather thin and 'run-down' just when the need is to be really fit and well. The result will be bigger feed bills overall, quite apart from the pony's suffering. Gross underfeeding can amount to cruelty.

If you are unfortunate in that the grazing on your pony's paddock is very sparse, it may also be necessary to feed hay in summer. As an alternative, you may prefer to feed cut grass. So long as you feed only really fresh grass this is unlikely to do any harm, though you should be sure to remove any wilted material. This is liable to give the animal colic, particularly if the grass has decomposed so far that it has begun to heat up. Lawn mowings are extraordinarily dangerous in this respect as they begin to ferment very rapidly in the pile. Also, being relatively fine, they tend to impact in the pony's stomach, especially if the animal is greedy and scoffs them down without chewing them. Large quantities of lawn mowings should therefore be consigned to the compost heap and not given to the pony.

The trend in modern farming is towards silage production, and big bales. This means that good quality hay, in manageable small-sized bales, is becoming less widely available and more expensive. Hence, horse owners have been increasingly looking for alternatives to hay. Horses will readily eat silage, and various vacuum packed silage-like cut grass products are now commercially available specifically for horses ('haylage', 'horshage'). Although they will eat 'big bale' silage, this is not recommended. There have been several fatalities due to contamination of this form of silage with botulism, following puncture of the bags by rats. If the bag of any of these horse silage products has been punctured, or the contents smell of ammonia, they should not be fed.

Other alternatives to hay include grass or lucerne cubes. So-called complete rations are also available. These make the feeder's task simpler by incorporating the fibre content of the diet (usually in the form of treated straw) into the cubes to provide a balanced ration.

8

EXTRA FOOD

The outdoor pony eats the grass in the summer, and in winter eats the same thing in the form of the hay which is given instead. Grass is the natural food. But if the pony is working hard or the weather is bad there will be a need for something besides grass and hay to give energy and warmth. The extra feed should be grain, or horse nuts, or one of the wide variety of other pony foods which – being less bulky than grass and hay – are collectively called 'concentrates'.

These foods are usually given as a special 'feed' in a bucket, manger, or feed bowl. This is an artificial form of feeding, very different from the pony's natural way of eating. Further, the equine digestive system is remarkably easily upset. Wrongly fed concentrates can produce 'colic', a severe belly ache with serious, and potentially fatal complications. If the pony is to derive maximum benefit from the extra food (as well as most enjoyment) without risk to health, it has to be fed with skill and care. The following ten are the most important 'principles of feeding'.

1 – *Feed Plenty of Roughage*
The wild pony eats grass, and lots of it. The domesticated pony also needs the fibre that grass or hay provides. Digestion is more efficient if the pony has to chew food thoroughly and this is encouraged by mixing 'chaff' with the grain ration. 'Chaff', sometimes called 'chop', is good quality hay which is put through a chaff-cutting machine. Not a very complicated device, this consists of a chute with a huge blade, turned by hand, cutting the hay into lengths of 1–2 inches (2.5–5cm). Buying chaff ready-cut is a mug's game, however, unless you can be sure that rough old hay has not been used for it. If you cannot borrow a cutter, bran is another good form of roughage to mix with your pony's oats.

The gut of herbivores is adapted to function best if it is always full of roughage, which brings us to the next point . . .

2 – *Give Small Feeds Often*

A pony's eating habits differ greatly from those of a human being. We prefer to eat our food in three or four daily meals. Dogs carry this still further, for they will happily eat just one colossal meal a day, or even one every two days. This is partly because dogs have stomachs which will stretch enormously. A pony by contrast, has only a very small and inelastic one, so munches steadily for most of the time, stopping only for an occasional doze, or when out for a ride.

If the pony goes without food for a time and then gobbles a large meal, the stomach is stretched severely and may not be able to hold all the food. The result is that the animal develops colic. For a pony living indoors all the time the daily ration should be divided into at least three feeds, and preferably four, per day. A pony living out of doors may get only one concentrate feed per day, plus hay, but is eating grass for much of the rest of the time.

3 – *Feed Good Food Only*

Ponies do not thrive on poor quality, old, stale or mouldy food and it may do them serious harm. Many animals will not eat it but occasionally a piggy pony gobbles up, for example, mouldy hay. As a result the unfortunate animal may spend a most uncomfortable night with colic, and the owner may pass a very worrying one. Anyway, poor grade feed seldom has much nutritive value. It may be cheaper to buy in the first place, but you will have to feed much more to get the same result. The cost is the same, or even more, in the long run.

4 – *Feed According to Exercise*

Ponies are very good at regulating their own intake of hay. After eating a certain quantity there is simply no room for more and so the rest is left, though it may be eaten later. This is one of the reasons why hay is such a valuable food for ponies and one with which, provided it is of good quality, it is hard to make serious mistakes in feeding.

The commonest concentrates fed to horses are oats, flaked maize, barley, sugar beet and various types of horse cubes/nuts. These provide the energy needed to keep warm in the cold weather, to perform work and to improve a pony's condition if it is rather thin and 'poor' so that it needs energy just to live. Thus

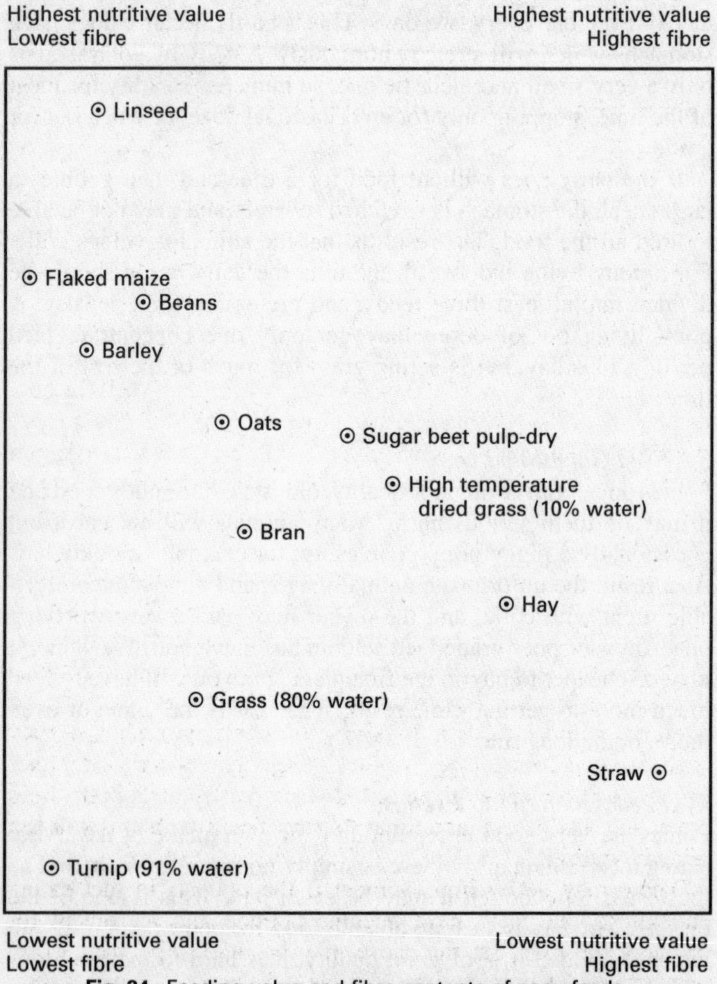

Highest nutritive value
Lowest fibre

Highest nutritive value
Highest fibre

⊙ Linseed

⊙ Flaked maize
⊙ Beans

⊙ Barley

⊙ Oats
⊙ Sugar beet pulp-dry

⊙ High temperature
dried grass (10% water)

⊙ Bran

⊙ Hay

⊙ Grass (80% water)

Straw ⊙

⊙ Turnip (91% water)

Lowest nutritive value
Lowest fibre

Lowest nutritive value
Highest fibre

Fig. 24. Feeding value and fibre contents of pony feeds.

it is reasonable that in cold, hard, weather or if being ridden a lot, especially in winter, a pony needs concentrates as well as hay and grass.

There are one or two exceptions to this. Concentrates will tend to make a very small pony unmanageable unless working extra-ordinarily hard. For the same reason, it is unwise to give 'hard food' to a pony which is already rather naughty and difficult to cope with. An adequate ration of good quality hay is usually sufficient for such animals. Occasionally a few horse nuts may be fed, if the weather is very bad, for example, as these do not seem to have the exciting effect of most other feeds.

5 – *Feed According to Condition*

The drains being made on the pony's energy reserves (due to cold weather, hard work, illness) give you an idea of roughly how much you should feed in the way of concentrates. The condition of the pony allows you to make fine adjustments to the food. If the animal is looking well, seems full of energy, is alert and interested, with a shiny coat (the winter coat should glisten as well as the summer one) and is reasonably plump (so that you can only just feel the ribs) then the pony is probably being fed about right. If thoroughly naughty or too stout, or both, the pony is having too much. The first thing to reduce, and perhaps cut out completely, is the 'concentrate' ration. The hay or grass intake may be reduced a little, if necessary, later.

If the pony is too thin, on the other hand, something has to be done, as not enough food is being consumed. A pony is said to be 'poor' if ribs are easily visible, the coat is stark and staring, the animal seems to lack energy, vitality and interest in what is going on around, and tends to stand 'tucked up' (see fig. 25 overleaf) with head down, looking thoroughly miserable. A pony may lose condition simply for lack of enough decent food, either because it is not being given or because other animals in the field are eating that particular animal's share. These problems you can remedy yourself.

There may be no improvement if the pony is in fact eating enough but the teeth have become pointed and inefficient for grinding the food. Or the cause may be infestation with worm parasites, or the pony may be ill. If any of these problems are sus-

Fig. 25. If the pony stands 'tucked up' . . .

pected, the sooner you get your veterinary surgeon to come and
have a look at the pony the better.

6 – *Water Before Feed*
Ample supplies of good clean water are essential if a pony is to
thrive and it is best if fresh water is available all the time. If for
any reason it is not, or if you have just returned from a ride, offer
a long drink – as much as the pony wants – before giving the feed.
The reason for this is that water passes more rapidly through the
front parts of the pony's gut. If feed is there already, a sort of traffic jam is created with the water pushing from behind. The result
may be painful for the pony, with a lot of stretching of that sensitive intestine, and the colic may be severe.

Problems arising from horses being given a long drink after a
meal are fewer than formerly. In the old days, trade horses were
kept in rows of stalls and brought out to drink at a communal
water trough. A horse would come in from work hungry and tired,
to be given fodder and consume it while the van and harness were
being put away. Then, perhaps as he was going home, the driver
would remember that he hadn't offered his unfortunate horse a
drink. The thirsty animal would gulp down a large quantity of
water and digestive trouble would ensue for the horse – and a tick-
ing off for the driver.

7 – *Let the Pony Eat in Peace*

It is a sound rule to feed the pony last thing before you go indoors yourself. Eating is a very important business to all animals and they hate to be disturbed by people rushing round, grooming them, or moving other animals about. A pony may also, probably without thinking, lash out unexpectedly if touched when eating, so is best left alone.

If you must watch the animal eat, do so from a good distance, from outside the stable or paddock. It is better to go away and return half an hour later to see if the food has been finished.

8 – *Feed All the Ponies*

Ponies' tempers can become very short at feeding times and even the best of friends will kick out viciously at, and possibly even injure, one another as they mill about. Never feed just one pony, or leave one out when you feed several. This is just asking for jealousy. If only one animal is to be fed, take the pony out of the field and out of sight and smell of the others to give the meal. Sometimes one pony has to be left out. This animal should be given a 'pretend' feed, a bucket with a handful of bran and chaff or something of the sort, to keep occupied while the others eat.

As well as providing one feed bowl and one hay net per pony

Fig. 26. Let the pony eat in peace . . .

you should ensure that each bowl and net is out of range of any other pony. If this is not done, a powerful character is likely to get double portions while the shy animal goes without.

9 – *Work Before Food*
A pony takes one and a half to two hours to digest a full-sized meal and, like you, gets a pain and an uncomfortable feeling if strenuous exercise is taken on a full stomach. So you should always give a feed on return from a ride, never just before going out.

A 'feed' in this context includes a period of grazing, or a net of hay, as well as concentrate feed. The pony should be shut in without food (only water) for at least an hour before being taken out. If you have absolutely nowhere to shut or tether the animal away from the grass, then walking slowly for the first forty minutes of your ride will help.

Making a horse gallop when full of food can bring considerable discomfort. Among the signs of distress are laboured breathing, excessive sweating and reluctance to move further. Abdominal pain is indicated by kicking at the belly with a hind hoof and looking round suspiciously at the quarters. If distress is severe, try leading the pony around at a walk for twenty minutes or half an hour. If there is no improvement in this time, the vet should be called.

10 – *Feeding Routine*
All animals prefer to be fed at the same time each day. They soon come to expect their meal then – and are standing at the gate or hanging over their stable doors waiting. Patience may run out if the food is late.

The main feed of concentrates and hay is usually given at night so that the pony has plenty of time to eat and digest it. As nighttime is the coldest part of the twenty-four hours, the warming effect of the food is of most benefit then, especially to ponies living out of doors. A second feed is best given in the early morning and, for stabled animals, a third is given at midday and a fourth at about 4 pm. The routine has to be adjusted to suit the timetables of the humans who do the work, and to fit in with the animal's exercise.

If the feeding routine has to be changed it should be done gradually. This applies both to alterations in the time when the food is given and to changes in the feed itself; for example from oats to pony nuts, or the addition of one or more new ingredients to the diet. The keyword in all these changes is caution, for a pony's digestion can very easily be upset by a new feedstuff, albeit a conventional horse food of good quality.

Oats for Ponies

The traditional grain for horses and ponies is oats, which are given either whole or bruised by crushing or rolling in a mill. There is much to be said for feeding oats whole, unless you have your own crushing machine. The nutritive value of the grain begins to deteriorate rapidly seven to fourteen days after crushing, so this should always be freshly done. A normal, healthy pony with good teeth can chew whole oats as efficiently as crushed ones. The former have the added advantage that you can get a better idea of the quality of the grains. These should be plump and full, a good bright colour and a weight of 40 lb (18kg) or more to the bushel. There should be no stalks and seeds of weeds or pieces of earth among them.

Avoid oats with thin grains which have little or no room for a kernel (though a huge fibre content) and any batches where there is mould or greyness. This indicates that the grain has been soaked at some time, probably with rain. Chew a grain yourself. It should taste pleasant, not mealy, and slightly sweet. Oats, like any other grain, should be fed by weight. Most people use a measuring scoop whose capacity has been checked; any small bowl is suitable.

Flaked Maize

Flaked Maize is made by cooking maize and flaking and drying the porridge so produced. It is a nutritious food, as good in this respect as oats, though it tends to be lighter so that comparisons on a volume basis may be inaccurate. Like oats, flaked maize is best fed mixed with some roughage, either bran or chaff.

Field Beans

Beans are occasionally available as feed for horses and ponies, and are sometimes grown for farmstock in Britain. They are very highly nutritious. They should only be fed (and in small quantities) if the animals are using up a great deal of energy, either working extremely hard or living out in very cold weather. The beans, fed whole or split, should be introduced to the diet very gradually. You have heard the old saying that an animal is 'full of beans'. This is literally true since beans give a pony a great deal – often an excessive amount – of bounciness. Oats do the same.

Sugar By-Products
A by-product of the extraction of beet-sugar is the minced pulp of the beet which is sold for animal feed. Since it is marketed dry, sugar beet pulp must be soaked overnight in an equal volume of water to allow it to swell fully. If this is not done, the swelling will occur either in the pony's oesophagus (food tube in the throat) causing a 'choke', or in the pony's stomach and intestines, causing severe colic. Over half of the cases of 'choke' attended by veterinary surgeons are caused by feeding dry sugar beet pulp, usually inadvertently. Sugar beet pulp is nonetheless a useful feed for ponies, providing some roughage plus residual sugar, itself an energy source. It can be used to supplement or partially to replace a ration of oats or horse nuts.

Another by-product of sugar refining is 'molassine meal', a black, treacly-smelling meal which is sometimes used to supplement other concentrate feeds. It is sweet tasting and is therefore particularly useful as an addition to the diet of the faddy eater. It is also very nutritious and does not make ponies over-excitable.

Horse Cubes
Various compound feeds are available in the shape of cubes or nuts. These are specially formulated for feeding to horses and ponies. Many different types are sold; some 'stud' cubes have a high protein and energy content and are really too rich for most ponies. At the other end of the scale are cubes which contain a high proportion of roughage – fibre – and are designed to be fed as the sole food, with only a little hay or grass. Between these extremes are cubes which comfortably take the place of a mixture

of oats and bran and may be fed either mixed with these, mixed with just chaff or bran, or on their own.

Pony nuts are more convenient to give than oats and bran. The cubes are dense, take up little space and may be simply measured into the manger. The oats and bran, on the other hand, need to be mixed together, perhaps with chaff (which has to be cut) and then damped down with enough water to lay the dust.

Though feeding on cubed rations may sound easy, there are pitfalls. One of these is the need for ponies to eat some roughage with, or just before any cubes, except those high-fibre 'complete diet' brands. This is necessary because under an unfortunate combination of circumstances the cubes can pack down into a mud-like mass with which the pony's stomach cannot cope, except with additional roughage. The result could be a severe, or fatal, colic. Such a tragedy is averted by ensuring that the animal never bolts a ration of pony nuts on an empty stomach. There must always be some roughage, grazing or hay, to pick at before the feed, or else some chaff or bran mixed with the nuts. This roughage gets the pony's stomach 'going'.

Bran

Bran is a by-product of the milling of wheat to produce the flour we eat as bread. 'Broad bran' is the fibrous, outer husk which comes in quite large flakes – a quarter to a half inch in size. Sometimes it is hard to buy proper broad bran and the corn supplier can only offer a fine bran, which tends to be dusty and is not so good.

Whatever the size of the flakes, bran should smell sweet. It should show no signs of sourness, lumps or mould. Though it has some nutritive value, its main use in a feed is as a source of roughage. Mix it with oats or pony cubes in a ratio of about one to three or four. Dampen the bran with a sprinkling of cold water, to prevent the pony blowing the loose flakes out of the manger.

Bran may be fed to a pony in another way; as a bran mash. This is effectively partially cooked. It is therefore very digestible and suitable for a sick or convalescent pony, or one which is tired after a hard day's or week's work. The mash is made by putting about 2 lb (1kg) of bran plus a tablespoonful of salt in a bucket and adding to it enough boiling water to saturate it. It is then stirred

Fig. 27. Making a bran mash.
Left: Put about 2 lb of bran into a bucket.
Centre: Add enough boiling water to saturate it.
Right: Cover with a sack and let it stand until it is cool enough to feed to the pony.

thoroughly and covered with a cloth or piece of sacking while it soaks and cools.

Do not feed a bran mash until it has cooled sufficiently for your hand (or, traditionally, your elbow) to be immersed comfortably. The bran mash takes time to cool down, usually a couple of hours, and it is important to stir it well before you test the temperature. Pockets of scalding bran may remain which will give the pony a nasty shock if come upon unexpectedly. A few oats can be sprinkled on the top.

Linseed
Linseeds are the small, tiny brown seeds of the flax plant. They are reputed to put a shine on the coat of the pony and improve condition, especially in cold weather. It is essential, however, that linseed be thoroughly cooked before being fed to a pony: uncooked it is poisonous. The cooking process itself smells rather unpleasant and is best done in an old saucepan kept specially for the purpose.

The linseed – between 4 and 6 oz (about 150g) for one pony – is put in the pan and well covered with water. It is brought slowly to the boil and kept boiling for a full fifteen minutes (time this carefully). The heat is reduced and the pan is then left to simmer very gently for about six hours, more water being added as necessary, and then allowed to cool. It will set into a nasty looking jelly. This is enjoyed by most ponies and is fed mixed with bran to make a warm mash.

Barley

Barley should never be fed whole unless it has been well cooked (boiled). However, rolled or crushed barley can be used to replace part of the oat ration.

Micronized flaked barley is a form of barley that has been specially processed to make it more digestible. This and other forms of barley are sometimes used as a substitute for oats to provide variety especially if the pony concerned is one that 'hots up' and misbehaves when fed oats – barley being less 'heating'.

Before boiling, barley should be soaked in water for a few hours (not long enough for it to begin to ferment). It is then brought to the boil until the husk splits and the grains become soft (two to three hours). Boiled barley is very digestible and is normally fed mixed with bran and is noted for its ability to improve the condition of a pony which is, or has been, unwell. Barley fed raw may give a pony severe colic.

Oats may be boiled in the same way to make them more digestible for a pony which is poorly, or to make a change in the menu. Variety may also be provided by adding cleaned and cooked parings of vegetables such as potatoes, swedes, parsnips or turnips or raw cabbage or kale. Carrots and apples, cut carefully into fingers to avoid risk of the pony choking, are also appreciated. As an occasional treat, black treacle added to the feed will make it more enjoyable for a pony, as well as more nutritious. This process is particularly good for concealing any medicines which may have been included in the meal.

9

GROOMING YOUR PONY

The desire for a smart appearance is not the only reason for grooming a pony. There are other benefits to be gained. One is that in the course of grooming you will go all over the body and you will find, for example, any small injuries which might need dressing, or the beginnings of skin diseases such as infection with lice, or the appearance of 'cracked heels', which require attention.

When you brush the pony before riding, remove any mud from the areas beneath the saddle, girth and bridle. If this is not done, gritty particles may be rubbed into the skin by the tack and cause discomfort and perhaps soreness. Even if you are going for a quick ride and you haven't time to groom the pony thoroughly, make a point of brushing mud from the saddle and girth areas.

A stabled pony, living a confined, indoor life, needs a thorough daily grooming to tone up the whole body. Grooming has a massaging effect which improves the circulation to the skin and keeps the pony clean. The outdoor pony does not need daily attention to the coat, though also benefits from being well groomed whenever ridden.

Grooming Equipment
Grooming includes 'picking out' the pony's feet. For this you need a blunt metal hook, called a *hoof pick*, to remove any dirt or stones lodged in the foot. The dirt is scraped from the foot, beginning at the heel and working towards the toe, taking care to clean thoroughly the grooves on either side of the frog. Picking out your pony's feet should always be the first job done when grooming, to ensure that it is not forgotten. It is a task which should be done before going for a ride and again on return, so that any stones are removed before they can damage the foot. If a nail has been picked up or the shoe has become loose, it can be noticed and

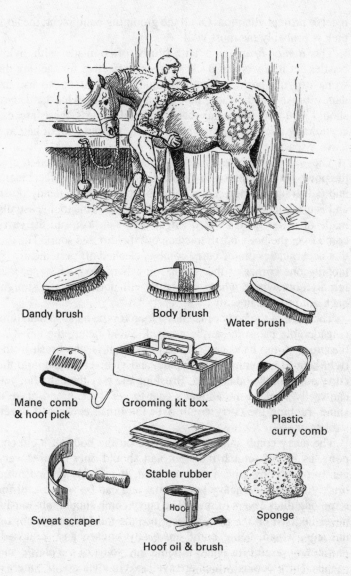

Dandy brush

Body brush

Water brush

Mane comb & hoof pick

Grooming kit box

Plastic curry comb

Sweat scraper

Stable rubber

HOOF

Sponge

Hoof oil & brush

Fig. 28. Grooming the pony; grooming equipment.

receive prompt attention. Of all the grooming equipment, the hoof pick is probably the most vital.

The *dandy brush* is a stiff brush, often made with nylon bristles set in a wooden back. It is very effective for 'getting the worst off' the pony, particularly mud. It is best not to use the dandy brush on the face, though, as it is somewhat hard. Nor should you use it on the mane and tail, unless these are exceptionally thick, as the stiff bristles will pull out a lot of hair and leave a sparse effect.

The *body brush* is less hard than the dandy and is used to give the pony's body a thorough cleaning, and to brush the face, mane and tail. It has shorter, rather softer bristles than the dandy brush and is used in combination with a *curry comb*. This tool is usually made of metal, with toothed ridges across it. You rub the curry comb over the body brush to clean out the dirt and scurf. The dirt that accumulates on the curry comb is cleaned off periodically by tapping one corner of the 'comb' on a hard floor or stone, preferably somewhere where the scurf will not be blown straight back onto the clean pony.

The back of the body brush has a loop for the hand so that quite considerable pressure can be applied. Stand facing the tail. Use the brush in the hand nearest the pony (that is, the brush in the right hand if grooming the left side, and vice versa) and hold the curry comb in the other hand. Brushing the way the hairs lie, you can really work at the animal's coat to get it clean and make it shine, rubbing the curry comb over the brush every half-dozen strokes or so.

The curry comb should not be used on the body of a clipped pony, as it will scratch the skin, and should only be used very gently on a pony with a summer coat. It may be applied more briskly to a pony's heavy winter coat and can be very useful for removing thick layers of mud. The curry comb should, obviously, never be used on the pony's head, nor the tail and mane, nor on the legs, which, being bony, are easily bruised and scratched. Particularly useful for outdoor ponies are some of the plastic and rubber 'curry combs' which are available in a variety of patterns. Being flexible these are particularly effective for removing caked mud and sweat from all parts of the pony's body and legs.

A certain amount of massage is given when grooming a pony

with a body brush, but a clipped animal, or one with a fine summer coat, will benefit from a 'wisping'. This consists of slapping
the pony's muscles with a wad of plaited straw, called a '*wisp*'.
You make this yourself. Begin by twisting a rope of damp hay six
or seven feet long. At one end of the rope two loops are made,
each about 9 inches (23cm) long, and the rest of the hay rope is
then wound tightly round the loops (see fig. 29). When it is finished the wisp is banged hard a few times on a flat surface, such

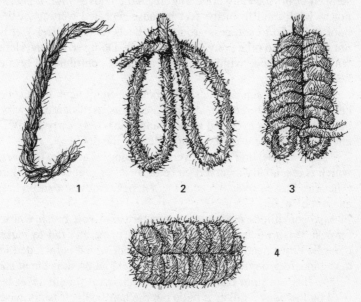

1   2   3

4

Fig. 29. Making a 'wisp'.
A rope is twisted out of damp hay (1); it is looped (2) and wound (3) to
make an oblong pad of hay (4).

as a wall, to make it smooth. It should be a comfortable size to
hold in one hand – about 8 inches (20cm) long and 2–3 inches
(5–7cm) thick. To use it, dampen the wisp and simply bang it
down on the pony's coat, in the direction in which the hair lies. It
is applied thus over the muscular parts of the neck, shoulders,
back and quarters; the pony may resent being wisped hard over
the loins, or actually over the spine. Wisping brings a good shine
to a pony's coat.

Instead of making a hay wisp some people prefer to use a dampened stable rubber folded into a flat pad in just the same way. A *stable rubber* is a piece of cloth about the size of a tea towel (an old one will do the job) which is also used to give the pony's coat a rub over at the end of grooming to remove dust and give a final shine. If the pony is entered in a show, its feet may be oiled as a finishing touch. Hoof oil can be obtained from a saddler and is applied with a small brush (such as a paint brush) – having scraped or brushed any dried mud from the hooves first. It is best not to wash mud from the feet because repeated wetting of the hoof may lead to soreness around the heels (cracked heels). It is not necessary to oil a pony's feet routinely. Doing so can interfere with water balance within the hoof and may contribute to brittle hooves.

A *sponge* is a standard item of grooming equipment. It must be kept clean and rinsed out in tap water. It is used damp to wipe gently the pony's eyes and nostrils and if it is very dirty a different sponge can be used for cleaning under the dock.

Useful for dealing with a very wet pony is a *sweat scraper,* which is essentially a curved piece of metal or rubber attached to a handle. Passed over the coat the scraper removes a surprising amount of water.

Also sometimes used is the water brush, a soft brush whose purpose it is to damp or 'lay' the pony's mane and tail to make them lie down neatly. A piece of equipment which is included in any standard grooming kit, but which is seldom used, is the *mane comb*. This is a stout comb, often of metal, but it should never be used on the pony's tail as it pulls out the hair badly. It is not wise to comb the mane much either, for the same reason, so that the only times when a mane comb should be used are when plaiting a mane or tail, or trimming them up.

The grooming kit is easier to keep tidy if one has a box or grooming tray to put things in. Alternatively, an old or perhaps leaky bucket makes a good container. All the grooming kit should be washed regularly in soap and water and the brushes, rubber and sponge dried thoroughly in the sun or beside a radiator. It is pointless to groom a pony using dirty tools as this may well put on more dirt than is taken off; it is also slovenly and may increase the risk of skin disease.

Grooming an Outdoor Pony

All ponies love to roll on the ground and they always seem to choose the dirtiest place in the field to do it (particularly if they are greys). A pony is usually rather muddy when first caught up even though the coat may be glossy underneath the layer of earth. The pony is wearing a headcollar and rope which should be tied to a suitable ring in the wall or a stout fence with – need it be said again? – a quick release knot.

After picking out the feet and scraping the worst of the mud from the outside of the hooves with the hoof pick, the next job is to remove the bulk of the mud from the pony's coat, using the dandy brush and perhaps the curry comb. If the fur is short it can then be brushed effectively with a body brush, paying special attention to the area of the saddlemark. It is sometimes said that a body brush should not be used on an outdoor pony's coat as it removes natural oil and makes the fur less waterproof. This seems unlikely under normal circumstances. In fact, a thorough grooming probably improves the condition of the coat by enhancing activity of the oil-producing glands of the skin, which is reflected by the hair's glossiness. However, a body brush may make little impression on a shaggy winter coat.

While you have the body brush in your hand, the pony's tail and mane are brushed out, from their roots and a lock at a time, so that the hair is cleaned and all tangles removed. This can be a very long job if it is only done occasionally. If the tail and mane are groomed often they loose the twists of hair or "rats' tails" and become easier to deal with. The pony's face is also brushed with the body brush. To do this the animal is untied and the headcollar buckled round the neck. Holding the head-rope in one hand, brush the face and forelock carefully, and sponge both eyes and nostrils before buckling the headcollar back in its normal place and tying the pony up again.

Next comes the massage with a wisp or folded, damp rubber and a final polish for the coat, though these may not be possible if the coat is very long and shaggy in winter. In summer, as a finishing touch you may like to apply some fly repellent onto the horse's skin which will help to discourage insects from being a nuisance whilst you are out riding.

In winter, particularly, you may bring the pony in wet from the field. It is impossible to groom the animal in this condition. The quickest way to dry the pony off is in a stable or shelter with plenty of deep bedding. Excessive amounts of water are removed first with a sweat scraper, and the pony is rubbed thoroughly with clean, dry straw. Then an old rug or a blanket of some kind is secured with a surcingle (a webbing or elasticated strap going round the pony's middle as a girth does), with a thick layer of dry straw underneath it. Loose stable bandages on the legs, also with a layer of dry straw under them, will help the limbs to dry. The object of the straw is to provide space under the clothing for ventilation and air movement. About an hour is usually needed for the pony to dry enough to allow attention with a brush.

'Strapping', 'Quartering', and Washing a Pony
Grooming a stabled pony follows much the same pattern as cleaning an outdoor one except that there is less time spent removing mud and more with the body brush and wisp. A full grooming is called 'strapping' and takes about an hour of hard work to do properly. A stabled pony is thoroughly strapped daily to keep in good health, improve circulation and help compensate for the long periods of standing still.

'Quartering' is the name given to the quick whisk over a stabled pony – or a clean outdoor pony – before going out, for example. The animal is not dirty and the quartering, with a dandy brush over the body and a body brush to tidy the mane and tail, just smartens up and makes the pony look presentable. It includes, of course, picking out the feet.

As far as possible, washing a pony should be avoided. It is never good for the animal and may be actively harmful; in winter there is seldom justification for deliberately wetting the animal's skin. As far as removal of dirt and mud are concerned it is always best to let the coat dry and then brush it clean. Washing the fur tends to remove some of the natural, healthy oiliness which gives it shine. This spoils the look of the animal.

Occasionally in summer a pony is washed before some special function such as a pony show, particularly if the animal is white or has white legs which become stained. The smallest area possible should be wetted, and washed either with household soap, or a medicated animal shampoo, and not with a detergent. Great care is necessary to ensure that all the soap is rinsed out. A pony's tail is washed most easily by dipping it into a bucket of warm water, soaping it and then dipping it again to rinse it.

Once washed, the pony must be dried as rapidly as possible. Start with the sweat scraper. Follow this by rubbing over with straw and then putting a sheet and bandages on with straw underneath them. If the weather is hot and sunny, a pony walked around in the sun will dry off just as well. One harmful effect of washing a pony is chapping of the skin in 'Mud Fever'. This is traditionally due to lazy grooms washing the mud off horses' legs instead of waiting for it to dry and brushing it off. 'Cracked' or 'Greasy' heels – soreness in the heels with an accumulation of lardy skin secretion round it – are chiefly due to the animal's legs being repeatedly wetted and not dried properly.

The Mane
Routine attention to the pony's mane has already been described. The mane looks neatest if it falls all to the same side of the neck, usually the offside. Repeated brushing helps to make it lie flat but sometimes this is not enough and the hair continues to grow in all directions. A remedy for this is to wet the mane and then plait it into pigtails which lie to the appropriate side, leaving the plaits in overnight. Some ponies do, however have such naturally bushy manes that it is hard to make them look neat; this is particularly likely if the mane has at some time been 'hogged'.

A mane that is too thick is thinned by 'pulling'. This is done when the mane has been thoroughly brushed, by taking a few – usually the longest – hairs at a time from underneath and pulling them out quickly with your fingers, or by winding them round a mane comb. This is continued until the mane is thinned as much as you want. Ponies seldom seem to object to the procedure unless too many hairs are pulled at the same moment.

A mane which is too long is also shortened by 'pulling' – never by cutting with scissors, which will spoil its appearance. The long hairs are simply plucked to the required length, usually about three inches, but this is very much a matter of taste. Some pony-owners prefer to let their animal's manes grow very long, and do nothing more than thin them, if that. But however short the rest of the mane is, the forelock should be left long enough and thick enough to give some protection from flies in summer.

'Hogging' a mane is really taking the shortening and thinning processes to the extreme as it involves complete removal of the mane with clippers. This saves grooming and looks smart on a cobby animal. Hogging is not recommended, however, for ponies kept wholly out of doors, as their manes provide some protection from the weather. Before a mane is hogged it should be reasonably clean and dry. The sides are dealt with first, then the middle part of the mane. Whether the forelock is left or not is a matter of taste, though its protective value from flies should not be forgotten.

Some people like to 'hog' short stretches of a pony's mane. This is not as peculiar as it sounds as the stretches concerned are about 2 inches (5cm) at the poll, where the bridle's headpiece lies and the mane may get very knotted, and from 2 to 4 inches (5–10cm) at the pony's withers where the hair may get in the rider's way and become tangled with the reins. Like a completely hogged mane, these short stretches require quite frequent clipping to keep up with the growth of the hair.

For a special occasion, such as a pony show, it may be desired to plait a pony's mane. This should be done with the mane clean and well brushed. You need a comb, a water brush, a pair of blunt-ended scissors, a reel of linen thread to match the mane and a blunt, thick needle. Instead of a needle and thread, rubber bands can be used to secure the plaits but they do not give such a smart finish.

The mane is dampened with the water brush to make it more manageable and divided into about seven separate locks. The first lock is plaited tightly to make a pigtail, a thread being included in the lower part of the plait. The end of the plait is tied round with the thread, to stop it from coming unplaited. Then the plait is wound up so that it forms a small, tight knob at the root of the hair. It is secured thus with the thread, using the needle to draw it through and through. The thread is finally tied off and cut short.

The Tail

The tail is normally brushed, like the mane, from the roots, lock by lock. The end of the tail hair is usually cut off horizontally or 'banged' with a pair of sharp scissors. Many a pony-owner has

Fig. 30. Plaiting a pony's mane.
1. The hair is combed and made into a long plait, the thread incorporated.
2. The end of the plait is secured.
3. The plait is wound up to make a tight knob, and stitched in place.
4. The thread is snipped off, leaving pony with completely plaited mane.

shamefacedly produced a pony with a very short tail because it is all too easy to forget one simple fact. When a pony is moving, the tail is carried considerably higher than when standing still; this has to be allowed for when trimming it. It is easier if there are two people. One holds up the pony's tail in more or less the position in which it is carried when going along. The other gathers up the hair in one hand and cuts it straight, usually level with or about 2 inches (5cm) below the animal's hocks. It may improve the appearance if the line of the cut is very slightly upwards towards the pony's back legs.

The top of a pony's tail is often very bushy and untidy. This can be remedied by 'pulling', that is thinning out the hairs on the sides and upper part of the dock, leaving those on the top looking neat and tidy. The pony's tail is brushed first and a very few hairs at a time plucked out quickly from the underside. The use of scissors on the top of a tail has a disastrous effect on its appearance.

The effect of a tail which is narrow at the top and full below is enhanced by the use of a tail bandage. Made usually of stock-

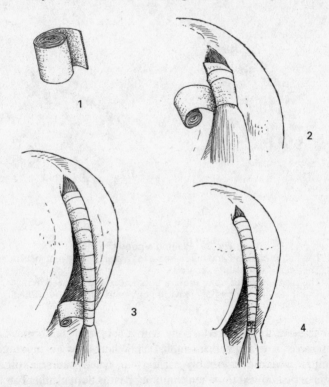

Fig. 31. Putting on a tail bandage.
1. Bandage rolled, tapes inside.
2. Starting at top of tail.
3. Working downwards.
4. Tapes tied below end of dock.

inette, the bandage is rolled with its tapes inwards and applied to the brushed and dampened tail (dampening the bandage directly should be avoided as the bandage may shrink and hurt the pony's tail). The bandage is applied from the top of the tail downwards, and firmly enough to prevent it slipping off, though not so tightly that it damages the pony's dock. The tapes of the tail bandage should always be tied below the end of the dock. Tying them round the dock itself could cut off the blood supply and lead – conceivably – to the end of the pony's tail dropping off. The tail bandage is removed by grasping it at the top and simply sliding it off the tail which should, after being bandaged for a few hours only (not more than six hours), be 'set' into the required shape.

Instead of 'pulling' and bandaging a pony's tail into shape its hair may be plaited. For this a tail with plenty of hair at the top of the dock is preferred. It is brushed thoroughly and dampened with a water brush. Starting at the root of the tail a small lock of hair is taken from each side of the dock and one from the centre. As far up the tail as this, the hair is short and only one cross-over of a plait is possible before more hair has to be taken up and plaited in. Thus, a plait can be made down the centre of the pony's dock. Lower down, the hair is longer and it is possible to make a long central plait which is doubled under once and then stitched in place (see Fig. 32, overleaf).

Trimming the Pony
Many ponies, particularly those of less aristocratic descent, tend to grow heavy beards and hair on their heels. This may not look very smart on an otherwise well-turned out animal. A beard of hair between the lower jaws is best removed carefully with scissors, though care is needed to avoid leaving cut marks. Alternatively, clippers may be used.

The whiskers on a pony's muzzle and at the eyes are sometimes removed, too, for a smarter look. This is unkind, however, to an animal which gets food by grazing – as the whiskers are used as sensors which tell how close the nose is to the ground. The hair inside the ears should not be removed, either, unless there is a large enough quantity to look very untidy. Then only enough should be trimmed to give a neat appearance. The fur is there to keep the insides of the ears warm.

The hair on the pony's heels may also be removed and in summer this is unlikely to do any serious harm. In winter a pony living out of doors is best left with a full complement of heel hair and this does not look too untidy. Some ponies grow only a little hair on their heels and this can be removed by plucking. Alternatively scissors or clippers can be used, though care is needed to prevent unsightly marks and unevenness.

When clipping the pony's heels do not forget that there is the

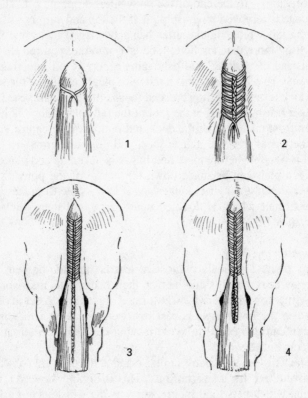

Fig. 32. Plaiting a pony's tail.
1. The first cross-over.
2. Working down.
3. With the long 'tail'.
4. The 'tail' is doubled under and sewn in place, to give the finished effect.

little horny 'ergot' at the hindmost point on each fetlock and this is very easy to cut accidentally. The ergot normally requires no attention. Its function, it has been suggested, is to protect the point of the fetlock when the pony's heel sinks so far as to touch the ground, as it may do when landing over a fence, for example. Occasionally action pictures of steeple-chasers or show-jumpers show this.

The function of the 'chestnut', the horny lump on the inside of the pony's legs above the knees and below the hocks is less easily explained. Generally the chestnuts need little attention, though they grow continually. Sometimes they become large enough to get in the way when the pony is moving, or to be in danger of being torn. If so the farrier may be asked to pare them down, or you may be able to peel off some of the outer layers without causing the animal any discomfort.

10

CLIPPING AND CLOTHING

A pony moults twice a year. It is most noticeable in the spring when a large quantity of fur is shed and the short, sleek, summer coat is grown. In the autumn these short hairs are replaced again by the longer and slightly more greasy ones of the winter coat. This heavy coat keeps the pony warm, and the oil in the coat helps to make it waterproof.

When the weather is very cold a pony's fur actually stands on end. This increases the layer of warm air trapped in the coat, and so improves the pony's insulation against the cold outside. It is just the same as a person who puts on an extra sweater to keep warm. This is why it is necessary to brush out any hairs which are stuck together in 'points' in the sweat-marks before the animal is turned out into the field. It enables the fur to stand up properly.

The pony can vary the degree to which the coat stands up and thus, to some extent, can control the body warmth. Even so, if working hard, the pony gets very hot and, because of the heavy coat, sweats a great deal. This can result in a loss of condition and – because the long coat is difficult or impossible to dry quickly – a considerable risk that the animal will become chilled. It is also hard to groom the winter coat thoroughly to make the pony look smart.

Removing the heavy coat with clippers solves these problems, and, if you intend to ride much in winter, it is really a kindness to clip the pony, at least partially. It does mean that, when not working, the pony has no protection from the weather and cannot keep warm For this reason the pony has to be provided with rugs, blankets, and other clothing to avoid getting cold while not at work. If clipped, the animal should be housed at night.

How to Clip a Pony
The summer coat, being fine and short, is never clipped. The winter coat is generally given its first clip at about the end of October. It begins to grow again at once and during January it will require a second clip; a third may be necessary towards the end of the winter. If so care should be taken that the summer coat has not begun to come through as clipping may damage the new fur.

Electric clippers are normally used to clip horses. These can be powered directly from the mains or from batteries or can be rechargeable. Simple hand clippers are available but are very hard work over a large area of pony. All clippers should have sharp blades and any hairs accummulating on them should be blown or brushed off at frequent intervals. The blades should also be kept well oiled during the clipping.

It requires some skill to clip a horse to look smart, with no unevenness or clipper marks. The clippers are used in the opposite direction to that in which the hair grows and with as level a pressure as possible. Few animals object to being clipped, provided it is done quietly and that the clipper blades are sharp. If they are blunt they pull and tweak the hair. The animal's coat must be clean and, as far as possible, free of dust and grease. Test for this by running the fingers through the coat against the fur. This will produce tracks of scuff if the coat is dirty. The presence of grit and grease in the coat greatly increases the wear on the clipper blades, which are expensive to replace.

The coat has to be dry before clipping, partly because the clippers do not cut damp fur well, but also because of the risk of giving the pony an electric shock. All clippers should be checked for their electrical safety anyway as, understandably, a pony which has once received a shock from the clipper head is dubious about being touched by it again. Some animals seem to have a deep natural distrust of being clipped, whether or not they have had an unpleasant experience in the past. If gentle but firm handling will not persuade such a pony to tolerate the clippers it is probably best to send the animal to a professional (with a suitable warning). In some instances the problem is so bad that it is necessary for the veterinary surgeon to give the pony a sedative before clipping can start.

Fig. 33. Various styles of clip.
(From the top) Clipped out, hunter clip, blanket clip,
full trace clip, small trace clip.

Styles of Clip

A pony which has had the whole coat shortened is said to be 'clipped out'. A 'hunter clip' involves taking off all the fur except that on the legs, which is left as protection from the brambles and thorns found in rough country. The saddle mark is usually left too. This is not done as a protection against the saddle galls. If the saddle rubs, it rubs and a layer of fur will not prevent damage to the pony's back. It is to prevent direct contact of a cold saddle lining with the pony's naked back, which could make the animal buck. Also, if the fur is left long, there are no short, bristly ends of cut coat to stick into the skin causing irritation and soreness. The saddle mark is usually left by clipping around the pony's own saddle, which ensures that the patch is a good fit. Remember that the long fur of the saddle mark requires drying when the pony comes in sweaty, as chilling of the skin may cause soreness on the saddle mark. This may put the pony off work.

A pony which is clipped all over requires a considerable amount of clothing. Such an animal will find it cold if turned out in the paddock for more than a short time on a winter's day (even if provided with an outdoor rug). The pony will have to be stabled most of the time and groomed and exercised thoroughly every day.

A simpler approach to the problem of the too-heavy winter coat is to remove it partially, clipping the areas where there is most sweating but leaving the rest of the fur. This reduces the amount of clothing the pony needs. The partially clipped pony can live comfortably outside by day wearing a waterproof rug, either coming into the stable at night or using a well-bedded down field shelter.

The most popular partial clip is *'trace high'*. The hair is removed from the belly, front, and up the gullet. It may be taken off the lower half of the pony's head and neck as well, though if more than the minimum is removed then correspondingly more clothing is needed. The *'blanket clip'* is an extension of the trace clip, or a reduction of the hunter clip, depending on which way one looks at it; it involves removal of all the fur except that on the legs and an area like that covered by a small rug thrown over the pony's back.

Clothing

Clothing is needed in winter to replace the coat of the clipped pony and, occasionally – such as when ill – an unclipped pony may need a garment to keep warm, too. The basic item of clothing is the rug. This should fit loosely round the animal's neck so that the head can be lowered comfortably to eat. It should not be so loose that it slips back and chafes at the withers. Rugs are cut so that they fit and allow room for the pony's withers and rump, but they generally need to be secured by a 'roller' or a 'surcingle' around the middle as well. A roller is preferable as it has pads which fit on either side of the pony's back and ensure that no pressure is exerted on the spine. A surcingle is simply a long webbing or elasticated strap, the former sometimes being stitched to the rug appropriately.

Putting a rug on a pony is called 'rugging up'. The back half of

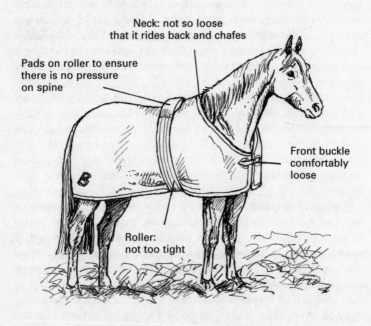

Neck: not so loose
that it rides back and chafes

Pads on roller to ensure
there is no pressure
on spine

Front buckle
comfortably
loose

Roller:
not too tight

Fig. 34. The fit of rug and roller: a day rug.

the rug is first folded forward over the front half and the whole rug is then gathered up in the right hand. Standing at the pony's near or left-side shoulder, throw the rug gently over the withers so that the neck of the rug is well forward of its eventual position. This allows it to be pulled back into its proper place, ensuring that all the animal's hair lies flat. The front buckle of the rug is done up and the roller put on so that it lies in the same position as a girth. It should be buckled looser than a girth, so that it is not uncomfortable, and it helps if the lower edge of the rug can be pulled out a little so that there is no tightness over the 'point' of the shoulder, which might be rubbed and made bald.

The rug is correctly positioned when its central seam lies straight along the animal's back. To remove the rug just undo the front buckle and the roller, fold the front half of the rug back and sweep the rug and roller back over the pony's tail, leaving the fur smooth and flat. The rug is then put out of the way in a dry corner of the stable, preferably somewhere off the ground.

There are a number of types of rug, used for different purposes. All are expensive and deserve proper care. This means periodic washing, scrubbing or dry cleaning to clean the fabric. The leather of straps and buckles should be thoroughly oiled regularly. All rugs should be thoroughly aired before they are put on the pony, for a wet or damp garment is often worse than none at all. When the rugs are stored, during the summer for example, they are best put away – clean – with moth balls, in a suitably dry cupboard or chest.

The 'Night' Rug

Traditionally, these were made of jute with a blanket lining and had their own webbing roller or surcingle. They are relatively inexpensive but hard to keep clean as they are easily soiled. Nowadays, most night rugs are made of quilted nylon and are held in place by straps around the legs or by a surcingle or roller. They can easily be washed in a washing machine. On a fine day the night rug will benefit from an airing in the sunshine.

'Blankets'

Under the rug varying numbers of blankets may be used to keep the pony warm in very cold weather. A proper horse blanket is

Blanket turned back
over front of rug

'Anti-cast' roller

Fig. 35. Night rug and blanket.

made of pure wool, fawn in colour with wide longways stripes at
the edges. Very smart, it tends to be rather expensive and many
people find that ordinary blankets serve the purpose almost as
well.

To put a blanket on a pony, fold it in the same way as the rug,
but throw it over so that the front edge of the blanket comes well
up the animal's neck. The back edge is then drawn back only as
far as the root of the tail and the rug put on in its normal final position. The front buckle of the rug is fastened and the front part of
the blanket folded back over the neck of the rug to make a 'fur
collar'. The roller is put on last. If more than one blanket is to be
used under the rug they are usually all folded back in the same
way.

But how do you know whether a pony needs blankets, or even
a rug? A reasonable guide is that a clipped animal, indoors, will
need no rug if the temperature is over 15°C (60°F), one rug if it is
between 7° and 15°C (between 45° and 60°F), a rug and one thick

blanket if it is between minus 1° and plus 7°C (30° and 45°F) and a rug and two blankets if the temperature drops below minus 1°C (30°F). A pony which is trace-clipped and stabled usually needs one less blanket than a clipped-out animal.

The temperature by which to judge how much clothing a pony needs should be the lowest reached during the night, as that is when the animal will really feel the cold. However, the guide given is only an approximate one and the final decision should depend on whether the animal is too hot or too cold. The best criterion is the temperature of the ears; they should be warm right to their tips. If they are cold then an extra blanket is indicated. Rub the pony's ears gently too. This seems to have the effect of warming and cheering up the pony. If the pony is too hot, on the other hand, sweat may be apparent; the damp patches will be obvious. Don't forget that the pony which has just come in from exercise or has not long finished a meal will probably be warm even though the animal may cool down considerably later.

The 'Day' Rug

For many ponies – or their owners – this is a luxury item. Made of a thick coloured woollen fabric, bound with contrasting braid and with the owner's initials in one corner, it looks very smart but is undoubtedly an unnecessary expense. The day rug is put on the pony which is standing in the stable to be admired during the daytime. It is held in place with either a roller or surcingle.

If the cost of a day rug is too much, it is perfectly satisfactory to use a night rug in the daytime, provided that it is not so thick that it makes the pony too hot on warm days. An advantage of having a different rug for the daytime, however, is that it allows each rug to be aired in turn as it is off the animal. Though a day rug looks very smart, particularly if you take your pony to competitive events, it is not as useful as some other types of rug. The more important ones are really a night rug, a 'New Zealand' rug, a 'sweat rug' and some blankets, which all come higher up the list of priorities for the budget pony-owner.

The 'New Zealand' Rug

Many ponies spend much of their time outside during the winter and for them a 'New Zealand' rug is ideal. Made of stout canvas lined with blanketing it is waterproof and provides good protection from wind and weather. The New Zealand rug is the same shape as a normal rug, with straps at the front, but it also has straps passing round the pony's hind legs, which prevent its being dislodged if the animal rolls. It may have a surcingle too, though this is not necessary.

The New Zealand rug is too heavy for a pony to wear in the stable, and too hot. Indeed, when first put on the pony a new rug may be rather uncomfortable as the canvas tends to be stiff and this, plus the leg straps in an unusual place, may make it necessary to give the pony some reassurance until used to the garment.

The 'Sweat' Rug
A fairly recent addition to the pony's wardrobe is the sweat rug which is like a string vest and is made of cotton mesh. It is very useful indeed, particularly when the pony comes in hot and sweating, as it will allow the animal to cool off without getting chilled.

Fig. 36. A New Zealand rug.

It also reduces the chances of 'breaking out' into a sweat again later.

The 'Summer Sheet'

This is made of cotton and/or polyester. It is a very light-weight rug which is used to keep dust and flies off a clean pony in summer. It does not help materially to keep the pony warm, but a summer sheet is useful when a pony is being transported to a gymkhana, for example.

Being light, the back corners of the sheet are liable to be blown up by the wind. To prevent this, a 'fillet string', a light cord of plaited braid to match the binding of the sheet, is attached to the loops at each corner so that it passes above the pony's hocks, under the tail.

Leg Bandages

Bandages are applied to a pony's legs for a number of reasons; those used to protect wounds and give support ('exercising bandages') are described in Chapters 11 and 13. 'Stable' bandages are used to keep the pony's legs warm and are sometimes used to give protection when the animal is travelling.

Stable bandages are made of wool or synthetic woollen-type material. They are 7–8 feet (about 2 metres) long, 4 inches (10cm) wide, with tapes sewn to one end. It is not difficult to make a set of four yourself. Each bandage is rolled up with tapes neatly folded in the middle of the roll. It is then applied to the leg, beginning just below the pony's knee or hock and winding the bandage downwards round the leg. The bandaging is continued as far down as the coronet band. Then the bandage is applied upwards again so that the tapes can be tied neatly below the knee, with the knot on the outside of the cannon bone. The bandage should never be put on tightly, only sufficiently firmly to prevent it slipping off. Stable bandages are put on the pony as equine socks to keep the legs warm; they are particularly comforting to an animal which has had a long tiring day, which is ill, or is simply feeling the cold during very hard weather.

Bandages may also be put on a pony to prevent the legs being injured when travelling in a horsebox. A layer of cotton wool, gamgee tissue, or foam rubber should be put under the bandage, since a double layer of bandage fabric alone will not give very much protection. It is best if the padding can be extended sufficiently far down to cover the pony's coronet band, for this region is especially subject to injury from the opposite shoe. Even a small cut on the coronet band makes a mark in the wall of the hoof which takes a long time to grow out.

'Knee Boots' and 'Hock Boots'

On a valuable pony, particularly, it is a good idea to protect the hocks and knees, as these are vulnerable areas and may be injured

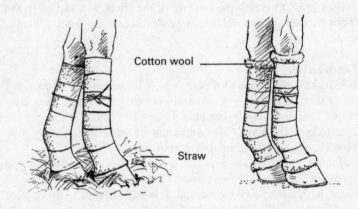

Cotton wool

Straw

Fig. 37. Bandages, for warmth in the stable (left), and for protection while travelling (right).

when the pony is travelling. The knee boot consists of a strong, stiff leather or plastic plate set in fabric with leather straps and buckles, or velcro fastenings, which should not be fastened too tight. The lower strap of the knee boot should be fastened very loosely below the pony's knee, so that the joint can be bent quite normally. This second strap is there merely to prevent the knee boot from being blown or turned upwards. The purpose of knee boots is to protect the knees from injury and consequent scarring ('broken knees') which would occur if the pony were to slip and fall on a hard surface.

The hock boot is similar in pattern to the knee boot. Its main use is to prevent injuries to the hocks such as 'capped hocks' should the pony back into or kick a hard object such as the stable wall or the back of the trailer.

A pony wearing protective leg bandages, knee boots and hock boots is rather restricted and should not be expected to go faster than a walk. The use of knee boots on young horses – and others – that are ridden on the road has become popular recently, though whether they in fact prevent many injuries is debatable.

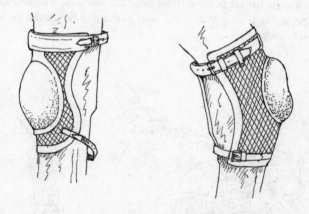

Fig. 38. Knee boots and hock boots.

Head and Tail 'Guards'

The risk that a pony may throw up his head and bang his poll in a horse box or, more likely, a pony trailer is the explanation for the use of the 'head guard'. This simple strip of padding, frequently foam rubber, is slipped over the head strap of the headcollar and should prevent the pony being injured or frightened if the head hits the roof.

The pony's tail is very liable to damage from rubbing against the back of the horse box, particularly if the animal tends – as some do – to lean the rump against the wall to keep balanced. A tail bandage is frequently used to protect the tail but a 'tail guard' may be used as well as, or instead of, the bandage. The guard is a piece of soft leather or thick woollen cloth shaped so that it can be wrapped round the tail. It is secured in place by tapes passing right round the tail and tied with neat bows on the outside. These tapes need not, and should not, be tight. At its upper end the tail guard has an adjustable leather strap by which it is attached to the roller to prevent its slipping off the tail.

For a clipped pony travelling in winter, a complete outfit could consist of a day rug, a blanket or two, plus travelling boots (or leg bandages with padding, knee boots and hock boots), together with a leading rein, headcollar and headguard, and tail bandage. However, for all but the most delicate animals, a headcollar and rope, a rug if it is very cold, and perhaps a tail bandage are the main essentials.

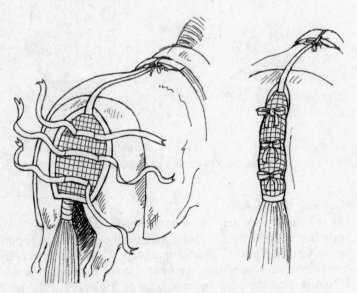

Fig. 39. Putting on a tail guard.
Wrapping the guard round the tail (left) and the guard done up (right).

Travelling Boots

Nowadays, there is available a wide variety of boots designed to prevent injury while travelling. They are usually made of synthetic material which encase the legs from just above or below the

Fig. 40. Ready to travel. Pony with headcollar and rope, sheet, tail bandage and guard, hock and knee boots.

knee or hock down to the coronet band. They are usually fastened with velcro and have the advantage that they can be put on and taken off quickly. Their disadvantage is that they have a tendency to slip down, so it is important to ensure that they are the correct size for the pony.

11

THE PONY'S TACK

The most essential part of a pony's equipment is the bridle and saddle. These sometimes have to be worn for long periods so that attention to their proper fit is very important. The fit is also crucial because you depend on the tack to control the pony. If you ride with weak, rotten, or badly-adjusted tack your life may be literally hanging by a thread, as may your pony's. On modern roads the chances of a runaway pony getting home in one piece are far from good.

Well-kept and properly fitted saddlery looks smart and enhances the appearance of the pony and, indirectly, the rider. The tack need not be expensive, nor even new: correct adjustment and good care have a far greater influence on the final effect than does the tack's initial cost. Furthermore, a pony loaded with all sorts of gadgets which are not really needed (such as fluffy noseband, a multi-coloured saddlecloth and a set of leg bandages) never looks

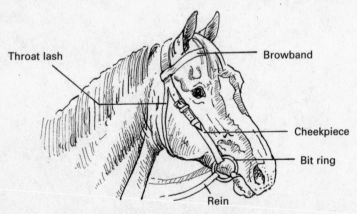

Fig. 41. The basic bridle.

as neat as an animal turned out wearing only the tack required.

The Bridle

The pony's bridle must keep the bit in place and provide some reins to give the rider contact with the pony's mouth. The basis of the bridle, and all that is strictly necessary, is the headpiece, two cheekpieces, a browband, a pair of reins and the bit.

The 'headpiece' passes over the pony's poll and on each side goes through a loop at the end of the browband. It includes a long thin strap, the 'throat lash', which is buckled under the pony's gullet and should always be slack – with about 3 inches (7cm) or a hand's breadth spare – so that the pony is not throttled when arching the neck. The 'browband' is a short strap with a loop at either end, and it is often colourfully decorated. A common mistake is to use too short a browband so that the headpiece is pulled tight round the ears. The function of the browband is merely to prevent the headpiece's slipping back down the neck. There should be room for a couple of fingers between the brow and the pony's forehead.

On either side of the pony's head the strap of the headpiece buckles to a short 'cheek piece', which is attached to the bit by stitching, a buckle or a stud fastening. The same range of

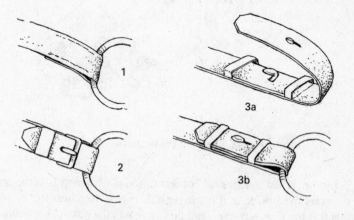

Fig. 42. Cheek pieces and reins are attached to the bit by stitching (1), a buckle (2), or by a stud fastening (3a and 3b).

fastenings is available for the reins, though usually studs are the neatest, longest lasting and generally most satisfactory. The reins themselves may be of ordinary leather, plaited leather, leather with leather lacing or rubber hand grips, plaited cotton or nylon or synthetic webbing (Continental web reins). Although plaited nylon or cotton is unlikely to break, it can cut into the hands especially if it is thin and the pony tends to pull. Most types of reins are quite satisfactory but many people consider that there is nothing to beat reins of plain supple leather and these are probably the best value for money.

The bit itself can be of several types, though the most common and probably the best bit for a pony is the 'jointed snaffle'. Made of metal (usually stainless steel or nickel) it has a jointed mouthpiece with a ring at each end to which the rein and cheekpiece are attached. The bit should be adjusted so that, with the reins hang-

Fig. 43. Fitting of the jointed snaffle.

ing loose, it just touches the corners of the pony's mouth. If the bit wrinkles the lips, then it is too high. It is easy to adjust the bit so that it is too low, however, and this increases the nutcracker action of the jointed mouthpiece. If you open the pony's mouth, the bit should be lying as shown in fig. 43. It should never be so loose that it bangs on the front teeth – a surprisingly common finding.

The thicker the mouthpiece the more comfortable it is for the pony. Some types of snaffle are favoured for this reason. It can be confusing that bits are called by so many different names although they all belong to one of the three or four basic types.

The jointed snaffle family includes the 'eggbutt' snaffle, which has a special junction between the end of the mouthpiece and the bit ring so that wear does not produce sharp burrs of metal which

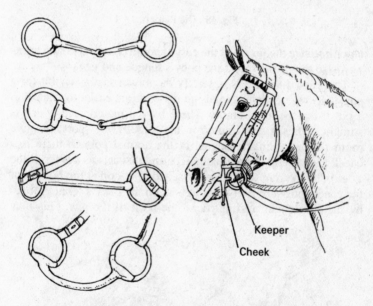

Keeper

Cheek

Fig. 44. Types of bit. Left (from the top): jointed snaffle, 'Eggbutt type', straight snaffle, 'Half-moon snaffle'. Right: 'Fulmer' snaffle.

can hurt the pony's lips. The 'bradoon' is a very simple jointed snaffle designed to be used with a curb bit in a double (two-bit-ted) bridle. The 'Fulmer' or 'cheek' snaffles have blunt spikes on either side of the mouthpiece. If you strap the upper end of the spike to the cheekpiece of the bridle, the bit is stabilised in the ani-mal's mouth. A further modification of the snaffle is the 'straight' snaffle which has rings at either end of a mouthpiece which is a round bar, straight or slightly curved ('half-moon snaffle'). In the

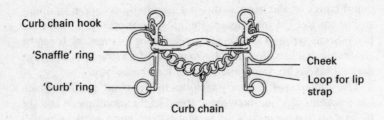

Curb chain hook

'Snaffle' ring

'Curb' ring

Cheek

Loop for lip strap

Curb chain

Fig. 45. The Pelham.

latter instance the inside of the curve should be upwards and backwards so that it fits round the pony's tongue and jaw.

The jointed snaffle is generally the most satisfactory bit for a pony. However, some animals go better or are easier to control in a bit of the 'pelham' family. These have a mouthpiece which is straight or has a small hump in the middle (the 'port') to give room for the animal's tongue. In the normal pelham there is a cheek at each end of the mouthpiece and this acts as a lever. If the rider pulls the rein (curb rein) attached to a loop at the bottom of the cheek, pressure is brought to bear on the pony's 'chin groove' by the curb chain passing round the back of the jaw. This may

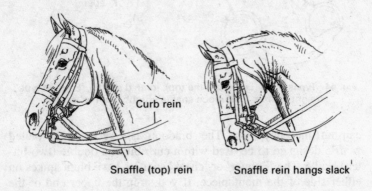

Curb rein

Snaffle (top) rein

Snaffle rein hangs slack

Fig. 46. The principle of the curb.
Tension, as the curb rein tightens, pulls back the cheek and tightens the curb chain of this 'double bridle'

actually be a chain or a leather strap or, sometimes, a chain fitted with a 'guard' of rubber or sheepskin to make the action milder. The curb chain is made so that it can be twisted to lie flat and it should always be used thus. It is attached to a hook on the bit and passes through the upper loop on the cheek (not behind it, where it would pinch the pony's lips) and then behind the jaw to the other side. The spare link in the middle of the curb chain should lie outwards; through it passes the narrow 'lip strap' which buckles on either side to the cheek of the pelham and keeps the curb chain in place. A lip strap is not strictly essential on a pelham, though it is correct to use one.

In addition to the lower (curb) rein, the pelham has a 'snaffle' rein attached to the upper loop on the bit, and this acts like a simple straight bar snaffle. Two pairs of reins may prove rather a handful so that sometimes short leather straps are buckled from upper to lower loops on each side of the bit and a single pair of reins used. The same idea is taken a good deal further with the 'kimblewick' pelham which has a straight mouthpiece with a port, a curb chain and a D-shaped ring to which a single rein is buckled so that its action is similar to that of a conventional pelham though somewhat milder. Though most ponies should be able to be controlled in a snaffle, a kimblewick bit is useful for those that take a strong hold.

Nosebands

Popular for ponies is the 'dropped noseband' used in conjunction with a jointed snaffle to improve the control afforded by the bit. Undoubtedly, many ponies go very well in this combination. The strap of the dropped noseband buckles below the bit, but it is important that the front of the noseband is high

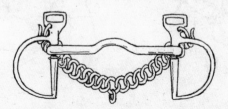

Fig. 47. The 'Kimblewick' Pelham.

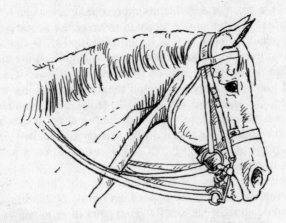

Fig. 48. The double bridle. A bradoon (a jointed snaffle) and a plain curb bit used together. Rather a mouthful for the pony and a handful for the rider.

enough not to interfere with the soft part of the animal's nose, where it might impede breathing and cause discomfort. It need not be buckled tightly, either, for its effect does not in fact depend primarily on the pony being prevented from opening the mouth.

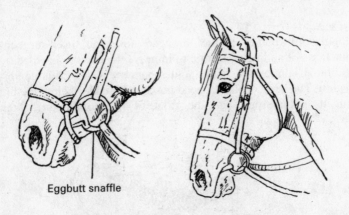

Eggbutt snaffle

Fig. 49. Nosebands. The dropped noseband (left) and the cavesson noseband (right).

The 'cavesson' noseband is like the dropped noseband in construction, though it is buckled above the bit and under the bridle's cheekpieces. Like the dropped noseband it is not an essential piece of tack, but is often added, through custom, to improve the bridle's appearance. The level of the cavesson noseband is adjusted so that it is about two fingers' width below the pony's cheekbone and it is buckled loosely enough to admit two fingers comfortably between it and the pony's jaw.

Bridling the Pony

Before worrying about how to put the bridle on the pony, one should learn to carry the bridle properly when it is off. The buckle in the middle of the reins is laid on the centre of the headpiece, which is the point held; this way the bridle does not get tangled up or dragged in the mud and is ready for putting on the pony.

The reins are put over the head so that the animal can be controlled when the headcollar is taken off. Standing on the pony's near side and holding the top of the headpiece in your right hand, bring the bit gently against the front teeth with your left. This will make most ponies open their mouths so that you can slip the bit in with your left hand. The headpiece is pulled carefully over the pony's ears, the mane arranged comfortably and the throatlash and noseband buckled up.

Fig. 50. Bridling the pony.

Occasionally a pony is stubborn about opening the mouth for the bit. Fortunately there are few animals which will not open automatically if you slip your thumb into the corner of the mouth just behind the front teeth of the lower jaw, though obviously care is necessary to ensure you do not get your fingers mixed up with the teeth. Most difficulties about bridling a pony arise from previous painful experience with the bit, either by someone shoving it into the mouth roughly or through its having rubbed sore places on the lips, gums or tongue.

Neckstraps and Martingales
The neckstrap is a useful piece of equipment for any rider, and one which makes the pony's life a good deal more comfortable. It is fitted in the same place as the collar of a carriage-horse. If the rider feels insecure in the saddle, going over a jump, for example, he can hang onto it instead of damaging the pony's mouth by pulling the reins hard. At its simplest a neckstrap is no more than a spare stirrup leather buckled round the pony's neck, though neckstraps are available which have a strap to the pony's girth. This prevents the neckstrap from dropping forward round the pony's ears when grazing. Any neckstrap should be fitted quite loosely round the pony's neck, both for the animal's comfort and so that the rider can take hold of it quickly and easily.

A martingale also provides the rider with a neckstrap, though this is not its prime function. The 'standing' martingale is a type frequently used on ponies. It consists essentially of a strap, buckled at one end to a cavesson noseband (never to a dropped noseband) and at the other to the pony's girth. On the way it passes between the pony's forelegs and through a neckstrap. The standing martingale prevents a pony from tossing the head in the air and banging the rider in the face, and stops the animal carrying the head so high that control becomes difficult.

The standing martingale should be adjusted so that it does not come into play until the pony has raised the head above the normal level. As a pony goes over a big fence, or makes an effort to regain balance after slipping or stumbling, the animal may need to stretch out both head and neck. It is sometimes difficult to adjust the martingale so that it serves its purpose without restricting the pony unduly. The 'running' martingale, which is similar except

Fig. 51. The standing martingale.

that it is attached by running rings to the reins and not to the bridle, does not restrict the animal in the same way, though it is less effective for controlling a chronic head-in-the-air. A most useful – near essential – adjunct to either martingale is a short, thick rubber band, available cheaply from any saddler. This is put diagonally around the slot in the neckstrap through which the martingale strap passes. It prevents the strap hanging loose between the pony's forelegs. This looks untidy and is more uncomfortable for the animal, which could also get a foot caught in the straps.

The Saddle
The saddle is the most expensive item of a pony's tack: it is often the hardest to fit, too. It is more comfortable for the rider to sit in a saddle than on the pony's bare back, and the saddle also pro-

vides attachment for the stirrups. A further and most important function of the saddle is to keep the rider's weight off the pony's spine. To do this it is constructed on a framework or 'tree', formerly made of wood but nowadays of metal, which has a central arch over the pony's backbone. The weight is carried on the saddle's padding, or 'lining', which rests on the thick muscles on either side of the spine.

A saddle which is too wide for the pony will hang on the spine like a Christmas card over a piece of string and nasty sores will soon result. You should be able to see daylight if you look down the central 'gullet' of a correctly fitted saddle, even when someone is sitting in it.

A saddle can be too narrow as well, in which case it will sit up – particularly at the front – and will pinch the pony's withers. Nothing can be done about this fault, except to replace the saddle. Nor can anything be done if a saddle is very much too wide for a pony, though where it is not too broad it may be possible to have the saddler re-stuff the saddle to make it a little narrower.

An alternative is to use a 'numnah', a saddle-shaped pad of felt, quilted nylon or sheepskin, or a saddle blanket, which is just an ordinary blanket folded to the appropriate size. This will sometimes help, as may a wither pad, provided one point is remembered. Every time you saddle the pony, the numnah or blanket must be pulled well up into the arch of the saddle so that it clears the pony's spine. If this is not done the numnah throws more weight onto the pony's backbone and just makes the situation worse.

The same applies to those saddle cloths and numnahs whose purpose is simply to keep the saddle's lining clean. Of several materials which may be used for the saddle lining itself, leather is perhaps the most satisfactory as it lasts well and is easy to clean. Serge, linen, and woollen fabrics tend to be less hardwearing and are very difficult to get really clean; a cloth may be used under them for this reason.

The saddle is held on the pony's back by the girth, a broad strap which is buckled to straps under the saddle flaps. Girths are made of a variety of materials. Flat or folded leather is expensive and has a tendency to chafe unless kept very clean and supple. Cotton, nylon string or synthetic (nylon and polyester) is also used; the

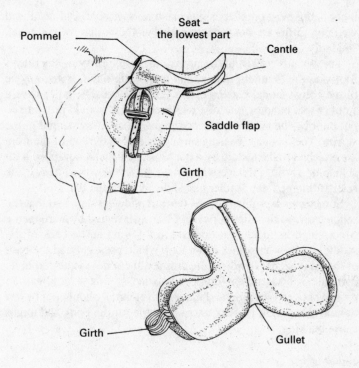

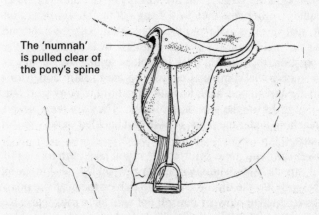

Fig. 52. The saddle.

latter being most popular as it is machine washable. Old fashioned webbing girths are not recommended as they often rot and break suddenly.

The stirrups consist of the 'irons', the frame carrying the rider's foot, and the 'leathers', the straps supporting them. Irons may be of the conventional pattern or the 'safety' type. The latter have a stout rubber band on one side which comes off should pressure be put on it by the rider's being dragged with one foot caught in the stirrup. The leathers, passing through a slot in the top of the iron, are attached to the saddle by a bar which is usually equipped with a snap-up fasting; this should always be left down so that, if the rider is dragged, the leather can slide back off the bar.

Sometimes a problem arises when a pony is shaped so that the saddle continually slips forward. This is prevented by a crupper, a strap which is buckled at one end to a D-ring at the back of the saddle. It has at the other end a loop which passes round the base of the pony's tail. To adjust the crupper, the saddle is placed in its correct position and the crupper buckled so that a hand can be passed between its strap and the pony's rump. It should not be too tight as this would be very uncomfortable for the pony and might cause bucking.

Saddling Up
Before carrying the saddle, run the stirrups up the understraps of their leathers, otherwise they will bang about. The girth is laid over the seat of the saddle and the whole thing carried over one arm. Put the saddle on the pony's withers, well forward of the proper position, then slide it back into place so that the fur underneath is smooth. Saddling and unsaddling are usually done from the nearside and so you have to walk round to the pony's offside to take the girths off the seat of the saddle. They are then picked up, by reaching under the pony's chest, and buckled loosely to the girth straps.

It makes the pony more comfortable if you take each foreleg in turn and stretch it forwards to pull any wrinkles of skin from under the girth. By the time you come to tighten the girth the pony should have stopped blowing himself out with air, a trick learnt by some animals which leaves them with a slack girth when the rider comes to mount. In fact, the girth never needs to be very tight and

Fig. 53. Saddling up. Stretch each foreleg towards you in turn, to pull any wrinkles of skin from beneath the girth.

you should remember that the best place to test its tightness is at the lowest point of the pony's chest; slackness down the side may be deceptive. Finally, fur under the girth is smoothed by running a finger down between the girth and the pony. If a folded leather girth is used, its free edge should be to the back as it will chafe and cut if it lies forward.

If a saddle cloth or numnah is used, this is put on in the same way, and drawn back into place so that it is smooth. The saddle is put on top of it. The numnah is pulled up into the saddle arch and the girths buckled before the straps or tapes which attach the numnah or cloth to the saddle are fastened. Where the pony's tack includes a martingale it is most important to check that the strap to the girth passes centrally between the pony's forelegs, as it may chafe if pulled to one side.

Cleaning Saddlery

Saddlery is expensive and deserves good care. The moment it is taken off the pony it should be hung on a suitable fence or door, out of harm's (and the pony's) way. Tack should be cleaned regularly, preferably every time it is used, to remove the salty sweat which damages the leather, and the layers of mud and scurf which accumulate.

Tack is best taken completely to pieces for cleaning. The bit and stirrups are scrubbed with warm water, dried and polished. The leather is washed with tepid (not hot) water and, if necessary, saddle soap (never detergent, which spoils the leather) to remove the coating of grease and scurf. It is allowed to dry, then a dressing of saddle soap or neatsfoot oil is rubbed well into the leather. This helps to keep it supple, repel moisture, and preserve the stitching. It is important not to use too much grease or soap and not just to smear it on over layers of dirt. It is a bad, but very common, practice just to wipe soap over the harness to give the surface a shine. If you look carefully you see the nasty thick coating of a black mixture of soap and scurf and grease and mud and grit; the last two in particular are bad as they will wear the surface of the leather and damage the pony's skin.

The girth, if it is made of synthetic material, can be washed in a machine and dried overnight. Alternatively, if time does not permit, vigorous brushing will remove dried mud and dirt. Webbing girths can only be cleaned by brushing with a dandy brush, and leather ones should be cleaned and oiled like the rest of the leatherwork, though it is especially important to remove any excess saddle soap from them. This also applies to a leather saddle lining. Other types of lining can only be cleaned with a brush (if wetted, they are difficult to dry properly). Sheepskin numnahs and girth guards are cleaned by brushing, whereas saddle cloths and cotton or padded numnahs are best washed in a machine.

The place where saddlery is kept is important, not only because of the risk of it being stolen but because air temperature and dampness have a great effect on leather. Ideally the tack should be hung on proper racks in a moderately dry atmosphere, such as that of a centrally heated house. If it gets too hot, as it would by a fire, for example, leather becomes brittle. Conversely, if kept in a very cold, damp place, it takes up water and acquires a sodden feel. In a warmish, damp atmosphere the leather will often grow large quantities of mould – an indication that it should be kept somewhere else.

While you are cleaning tack you should examine certain places which tend to wear badly. Bits tend to wear at the junction of the mouthpiece with the rings (snaffle) or the cheeks (pelham) which can cut the pony's mouth. The stitching of all tack usually has a shorter life than the leather, and it is worth remembering that sound leather can be re-stitched. Straps tend to give first at the holes, a good reason for undoing the buckles of the tack when cleaning it. It helps if you can throw the wear onto new holes by, for example, moving the buckle of the cheekpiece down on one side of the headpiece and taking it up on the other side to compensate.

Stirrup leathers tend to wear badly at the holes, especially if they are used persistently by one person. Periodically they should go to the saddler to be taken up a few inches at the buckle end. The girth straps on the saddle require watching for wear, and this includes checking the stitching of the straps at their upper ends. A 'buckle guard', which is a thin piece of leather, is usually fitted over the girth buckles to prevent their chafing the saddle flap, as holes in the flap are difficult to repair. With saddlery, as with so many things, prevention is better than cure. By keeping a watch for early signs of wear, serious damage can often be avoided, thus prolonging the life of the tack, and possibly preventing a nasty fall.

12

OUTINGS FOR YOUR PONY

Looking after the pony while out riding is just as important as attending to the animal's daily needs in field or stable. As far as the outdoor pony is concerned, being ridden may disrupt the daily routine built up round feeding times, regular spells of grazing, visits to the water trough and periods of dozing. If ridden only very occasionally, the pony might even feel that it is a bit of an imposition. On the other hand, many ponies seem to enjoy an excursion into the interesting world outside the field, even though it means that they have to work and may come home tired. This applies rather more to the animals which are kept stabled. These may, especially if there are no other horses in the building, suffer badly from boredom and loneliness.

Exercising the Pony
Ordinary work, such as just 'going for a ride', is sometimes called 'exercising' to distinguish it from special outings, such as pony shows, Pony Club rallies and other whole day occasions. These require extra preparation and effort, and are usually more taxing for both rider and pony. On an ordinary exercising ride both should return quite fresh as you are unlikely to be out for more than an hour or so, or to go very far from home.

You may choose to enjoy a daily ride along the lanes and bridleways ('hacking') or devote the time to training the pony in the field ('schooling'). Or, better, a bit of both. Most ponies seem to prefer hacking, which is less exhausting for pony and rider than intensive training. A short period of schooling, say twenty minutes every day, followed by hacking, will yield better training results than will an occasional marathon schooling session. This is likely to have no good effect, just frayed tempers on both sides.

On every occasion when mounted, a rider must wear a hard hat to protect his (or her) head should he fall off. (By law, riders under fourteen years of age are required to wear approved hard hats while on roads.) The hat must be a good fit and must conform to BSI 4472 specification – it should have a label bearing the 'kite' mark showing that it complies with the British Standard Institution recommendations and can withstand a substantial blow. The chin strap must always be fastened and be able to be adjusted for the individual rider so that it is not loose and cannot come off during a fall. Always wear proper footwear – jodhpur boots, not Wellingtons which are likely to get caught in the stirrups should a fall occur.

Increased motor traffic has made riding on the roads less pleasant and more risky. A pony which is frightened of motor vehicles is a dangerous animal, best got rid of regardless of other virtues. Much useful information on riding on the road is contained in the British Horse Society's booklet on 'Riding and Roadcraft'. In traffic, keep to the left and always make hand sig-

Fig. 54. You should observe road signs . . .

nals, as given in the Highway Code (get yourself a copy), to show other traffic your intentions. Observe road signs such as 'Give Way' as if on a bicycle or in a car. As the pony rider is going much more slowly than other traffic you should therefore, where possible, ride close into the side of the road and on the verge – unless it is a footpath or a mown lawn.

On the road the pony should always be kept under complete control. The reins should be held short enough to allow you to deal quickly with any emergency, such as a fright from a person appearing suddenly from behind a hedge or fence. Keep to a walk or steady trot as the road surface is very hard and jarring and may be slippery. Do not canter on the road, nor on the verges beside busy highways. If uncertain whether you can control a new pony, it is best to be safe and have someone accompanying you on a bicycle to start with.

Avoid riding at night whenever possible. If you do have to ride in the dark, remember two things. Firstly, the pony is most likely to be frightened by the headlights of cars as their light strikes quite ordinary objects such as trees and gates, and momentarily makes them look weirdly unfamiliar. This could make the pony shy suddenly into the middle of the road and the path of the car. To prevent this, use the right leg and right rein together, to bend the pony's head away from the cause of the fear. This also stops the quarters from being swung out. Secondly, you are in danger because you will be almost invisible to motorists. If you have to ride when it is getting dark wear fluorescent safety clothing with reflective strips on your pony and yourself (e.g. tabards, belts, arm or fetlock bands). Stirrup lights are also available. In an emergency, tie a white handkerchief to a stirrup or your pony's tail.

If it is possible to get onto a bridleway where there is no traffic to worry about then you can really relax. Bridleways are rights of way which enable riders to cross other people's land, and they are marked on the former Ordnance Survey 'One-inch' or the 1:50,000 maps. They are usually very pleasant to ride on. Spare a thought for the farmer and be sure to shut gates, walk quietly past farm-animals and as far as possible keep to the edge of fields sown with crops. If you wish to ride over land where there is no bridleway, for example in woods or over stubble, it is only civil to find out who owns the land and ask his permission before going on it. Footpaths, it should be remembered, are rights of way only for pedestrians and ponies may not be ridden along them.

Besides being enjoyable, daily exercising makes pony and rider fit. An hour's riding a day is the minimum for a stabled pony. It is important that the route be varied each day as the animal can easily become very bored with the same old roads and tracks. It takes some time to get a pony fit for really hard work and the daily exercise should increase gradually, with a corresponding build-up of the concentrate ration. When first starting work again after a long holiday, an hour of walking with a little slow jogging may be about all that can be managed. After a couple of weeks the pony will be able to manage quite long spells of steady trotting, and, after a month of regular work, should be quite fit.

If you have not been riding the pony for a time, for example during the school term, it will probably be found that both rider and pony will get fit together. Your own stiffness and soreness will tell you if you have ridden too far too soon, and it will give some idea of what the pony is suffering. It is worth remembering that lameness is often the result of giving an unfit pony too much work, particularly when tired. It is at these times that a pony is most likely to stumble and fall. Asking an animal to do more than he is ready for is thus a bad policy, as it can cause lameness for a long time.

It is sometimes said that an outdoor pony 'keeps fit' by wandering around the field. This is only partially true, for pottering round a paddock is a rather different matter from carrying a rider. The back muscles in particular become weak if a pony is not ridden for some time. Because of this it is particularly important that the unfit pony's back be rested periodically. You jump off for a few minutes. However, with daily exercise and probably some extra concentrates if very hard work is done, a pony kept out of doors should become very fit and ready for considerable exertion.

Special Occasions
Before the daily exercising ride, try to get the pony out of the field early enough to leave an hour or so without anything to eat before setting out. This avoids working on a full stomach. The pony needs to be groomed to give a tidy appearance, and the feet will need to be picked out. Before a special outing you will probably

want to do more than that to enhance looks and performance. Such occasions include pony shows and hunter trials, Pony Club rallies and hunting.

The Day Before
On the day before the event the pony is exercised as usual. Extra thorough grooming is required and in summer the mane, tail and legs may require washing if your pony is one of those characters which always looks grubby. After being washed, the wet areas should be scraped with a sweat scraper and rubbed dry with clean straw, and bandages and a rug put on if necessary (see Chapter 9).

It makes life easier if the pony can be kept in a stable overnight (so that there is no mud to roll in) and is ready waiting in the morning. A thick bed is needed for warmth, and hay and a feed overnight. On the day before the event, get the tack cleaned and ready, plus any other equipment which you want to take – or have someone else bring by car – such as a headcollar and rope, rug, bucket, and net of hay. Personal clothes should be brushed and laid out too, to avoid mad panics next morning in the search for lost gloves, sticks, or badges.

On the morning of the event the pony will require a feed early enough to leave at least an hour and a half between finishing the meal and setting off. The pony should be left to eat in peace, so it may be best to offer the feed, and then go away and eat your own breakfast. The next job is grooming. Some grey ponies have a knack of lying on the dirtiest part of their beds before shows so that they are covered with stable stains (often, it seems, they only do this when you particularly want them to be clean and beautiful the next day). Stable stains will be fewer if the bedding is deep and clean and if you go out and remove any droppings last thing at night. The only satisfactory way to remove the stains is to wash them off, wetting only the dirty area and drying it as much as possible with straw and a clean stable rubber or old towel.

The pony's preparation may include plaiting the mane and tail (though this is not usual for Pony Club rallies or hunting). Unfortunately this cannot be done the night before as the plaiting becomes loose and untidy if the pony sleeps in it. But with practice, you can become quite slick at these jobs. Time is also saved if all the materials, such as cotton, needles and scissors are put ready the previous day. The pony is groomed and made smart, right down to oiled hooves, and is left tied up while you go and change into your own tidy clothes and collect the tack. All you have to do then is to saddle and bridle the pony and you are ready to go.

Travelling

If hacking to an event, plenty of time should be allowed so that there is no need to rush. About 4–5 miles per hour is a fair speed to calculate on. If you are not very familiar with the route a map will be useful. This is not so much to tell the way – which is probably known – as to tell how far you should have got by what time. Seven or eight miles is about the maximum distance you could expect to hack to a show, rally or meet. This can vary according to the size and fitness of the pony – and the rider.

Travelling by horse box or trailer is quicker than hacking and is more and more common because of its convenience and the fact that the pony and his rider arrive clean and fresh. They can also stay late because there are none of the worries about hacking home in the dark.

Many ponies which are carried regularly by box or trailer seem to have absolutely no objection to the experience. Perhaps they realise that it saves a good deal of walking. Generally the transport vehicle is fitted with stalls, and an example of suitable dimensions would be a length of 6–8 feet (around 2 metres), a height of 7–8 feet (nearly 2.5 metres) and a width of about 2½ feet (0.75 of a metre). These measurements must depend to some extent on whether the pony is large or small.

A pony should generally be tied up in the horse-box, using a quick release knot, and a sufficient length of rope for comfort but not enough for there to be any chance of catching the feet in it. A net of hay, too, may help to keep the animal occupied during the journey. If it is a long one there should also be a stop to give the pony some exercise, a drink and a chance to urinate. Those not used to driving livestock transports should remember that the animals are travelling standing up and have to find, and keep, their balance. The speed at starting should be slow and driving should always be smooth and steady. A pony frightened by a rough ride may refuse to go into the box or trailer again.

The pony which is difficult to load is always a problem. A professional carrier will often get an animal into a box where others might fail. If no such help is available you will just have to do the best you can. Walking the pony straight in is likely to be more successful if you are looking ahead rather than back. A reward of food once in the box should make the pony easier to load next time. For ponies which persistently refuse to go in, a person on either side can use a long rope or webbing 'lunge' rein round the quarters to pull the animal up the ramp. This method is often effective, and the person at the pony's head should be prepared for the sudden decision that it is best to oblige after all. The pony may go in with a rush.

If a pony has once proved difficult to load, these doubts about the horse-box or trailer should be overcome gradually. This is best done by daily feeding in it; at first you may have to be satisfied with putting the feed just inside the box and watching the pony stretch the head in to eat, but slowly confidence will increase and you will be able to put the feed right inside. It is important that during this the floor of the box is well bedded down so that there is a good foothold. A sprinkling of sand is very useful for this purpose.

At the Event

You go to pony events to enjoy yourself, and ponies often seem to enjoy these gatherings too. They no doubt make a welcome change from normal routine and provide interesting contact with other ponies. Remember that they are naturally herd animals. But do not neglect your pony's welfare during the day. Do not use the pony's back as a grandstand for hours, sitting there chattering with your friends. Do not charge to and fro pointlessly, jumping practice fences over and over again. Treated like this ponies cannot reasonably be expected to give of their best when it comes to actually performing. By then they will be tired out and fed up.

Whenever you get the chance, get off the pony's back, run the stirrups up and slacken the girths. During a long day every animal should be given a proper rest, the bridle being replaced by a headcollar and the saddle taken off. The pony is then watered, either at the communal trough or, especially if there is equine influenza or strangles around, from a personal bucket filled from a tap. After a

Fig. 55. At a pony show, do not sit on the pony's back for hours . . .

long cool drink (enjoyed more without a bit in the mouth) the pony can either be held while grazing, or be tethered in a quiet place well out of range for kicking matches with other ponies. It is kind to give a net of hay to pick at while enjoying your own lunch.

Never sit on the back of a pony which is not wearing a bridle. Riding with only a headcollar, you do not have proper control over even the quietest pony. So you must resist the temptation to jump on the animal's back to return from the water trough, for example.

At the End of a Long Day

When the event is over the pony is likely to feel as tired, or more so, than you do yourself. The next job is to get both of you home as briskly as possible. If going by horse-box, the pony should be put in the box cool and dry, so as to emerge in the same condition at the other end. If hacking home then trot on steadily; with fairly short periods of walking, when it may be more comfortable for pony and rider if you get off and lead the animal. This stretches your own legs and eases the pony's back. Again, aim to bring the animal in cool and dry. Leading for the last part of the journey helps to do this. Slacken the girths for this last stretch, and move the saddle so that air gets between the lining and the pony's skin. Then the saddle mark should be dry, too, when you get home, and some rubbing down will be saved.

If the weather is good, so that the pony can lie down and rest outside, an outdoor animal is probably best put in the field for the night. Before this a quick brush over the saddle and bridle marks will restore the circulation and remove sweat and 'points' of fur. This makes the animal more comfortable, though one of the first concerns will, no doubt, be to have a good roll. The feet should of course be picked out before the pony is turned into the field, and any plaits undone. If the animal has had a particularly hard day, even in summer, it may be decided to give an extra feed. This meal should not be a big one, unless the pony is already getting a daily ration of oats or horse nuts, as the combination of an unaccustomed large feed with exhaustion provides an ideal setting for colic.

In bad weather and in winter the pony is probably best kept in for the night, so having somewhere comfortable to rest out of the wind and rain. Ponies are like people in feeling the cold more when they are tired. A feed and hay will be needed, though again not too much feed if the pony is unused to it. A check last thing at night allows you to make sure that the pony is neither too cold nor too warm, which is less likely. The former, detected by using the animal's ears as a thermometer, is remedied by giving a brisk rub down and putting a rug on – one is usually enough.

The following morning, whether the night was spent indoors or out, the pony should be checked over for any little injuries which might not have been spotted in the excitement of the previous day, and for lameness. Apart from this, the pony, and probably the rider too, deserve a day's rest.

13

VETERINARY CARE

Your main aim must be to keep your pony in good health, so that you do not have to spend time, effort and worry on nursing him during sickness, and he does not have to suffer the discomfort of being ill. Occasionally things do go wrong, however, but then your primary concern must not be to try to decide for yourself which of the vast range of equine diseases has struck. This is a job for the veterinary surgeon. It is much more important for you to devote effort to learning how to detect the pony's ill health in the first place so that you can call in the vet at the right time, early on in the course of the illness. The vet is the expert on the complex subject of animal disease and if a pony is sick then the sooner he is seen by a vet, the better.

Deciding whether or not to call in the vet is often problematic – particularly if you have not kept a pony before. It takes some time to learn to tell at a glance, as the experienced horseman can, whether a pony is well or not. On some occasions you may have a suspicion that all is not quite right but you may still be left with a nasty feeling of uncertainty. Unfortunately, there are no hard and fast rules which can be laid down on the subject. It is simply a matter of looking at horses and ponies under all circumstances so that after a while you know almost by instinct how a fit pony should look and signs of illness will not be difficult to detect.

Some signs help to identify the healthy pony. His eyes are bright and the animal is alert enough to notice anything interesting which appears, such as another horse passing by, or someone bringing some food. His coat has an underlying gloss, even though it may have an overlying layer of mud. The horn of his hooves has a slight natural shine, too. His fur should not come out in large amounts, leaving bald patches, although he will moult rather obviously in the spring, and again in the autumn. A healthy pony, though perhaps scratching the odd tickle, will not rub against trees and posts until areas of skin become thickened and inflamed.

A pony which is ill is miserable and looks miserable. He stands 'tucked up' with his head and tail down and his coat dull and staring because it lacks its natural gloss. His ears are at 'half-mast' too, neither pricked forward nor flat back, and they stay in that position. A healthy pony moves his ears continually to hear what is going on around. Often, sick ponies go off their food, though usually they continue to drink water. They are also reluctant to move and may feel very hot or cold, sweating patchily or shivering. In many cases, the first sign of sickness is that the pony becomes listless and will not graze or finish up its concentrates.

In a normal animal there is little or no discharge from nose or eyes, while in some diseases considerable amounts of watery or thick material may be produced. In the matter of puffing and panting it is often hard to decide whether a pony's 'blowing hard' is the result of exertion when he is rather fat and unfit, or is because there is something wrong with his breathing. Over-fatness is as often a problem with ponies as their being too thin because many pony owners tend to over-feed their animals. They are doing their ponies a disservice as a fat pony is not necessarily either healthy or happy any more than is a starved pony, and a reasonable medium is the aim. Remember that in a pony fatness is judged by the condition of the whole body, not just by the size of the belly.

Treatment of Wounds
Ponies, like humans, tend to acquire various cuts and scratches in the course of daily life. Small wounds generally heal satisfactorily with no more attention than washing the dirt away with clean, warm water plus a little mild antiseptic. Salt water (one dessert-spoon of sea salt to one pint of warm water) is one of the best natural wound irrigation solutions for flushing out debris and dirt from small cuts and scratches. This salt solution can be put in a hand-held garden sprayer, to keep handy in the stable for flushing and cleaning of such wounds. Avoid very strong applications such as the traditional tincture of iodine, which can often do more harm than good by damaging the delicate tissues of a healing wound. If something must be put on the wound after cleaning it, the best is

an antiseptic ointment of the non-greasy type you would use on yourself. Most small wounds heal perfectly well if they are left uncovered. If there is trouble with the area becoming dirty again, or with flies settling on it, then a clean bandage, loosely applied, may help, as may stabling the pony. Never use sticky plaster on animals – it sticks to their fur and is both difficult and painful to remove.

If using bandages to cover wounds, try to avoid the self-clinging, synthetic bandages. It is always safer to use a felt bandage, which cannot be applied tightly on the pony's leg. You should always pad underneath bandages with a clean, fresh piece of gamgee tissue or cotton wool to equalise the pressure over the pony's leg. Remember that small cuts and wounds may swell underneath bandages, and what was a properly fitted, snug bandage can rapidly become extremely tight during the night. This can cause the skin to die, because it becomes trapped between the swelling tissues of the leg and the bandage itself, and loses its blood supply.

Mild and superficial injuries can usually be dealt with using your own common sense; more serious ones may require the vet's attention. Four factors will help you to decide whether to call the vet in; how deep the wound is, whether it gapes when the pony moves, whether it is causing great discomfort and whether you are thoroughly worried about it. If the vet is to be called, do so as soon as is reasonable after the injury has occurred, but if possible keep calls to normal waking hours, for the vet's sake!

While waiting for the vet to come, an injured pony should be kept quiet. The injury is best left alone unless there is a danger of it becoming dirty, in which case cotton wool and a clean bandage should be applied. If there is serious bleeding, and especially if this is arterial (when the blood is bright scarlet and comes out in regular pulses) firm application of a thick wad of clean gauze or cotton wool helps to reduce the flow.

Apart from the wound itself, a further risk associated with injuries to horses is tetanus or 'lockjaw'. The second name is particularly appropriate, as an animal with the disease becomes progressively stiffer, with the jaw muscles the first to be affected. Tetanus is excruciatingly painful and untreated is a killer of ponies. There are two ways in which you can ensure that your pony will not be affected. Arrange for the vet to give him a course of immunising injections against it, before he has a wound. This will give him long-term protection, provided that booster injections are kept up, and it saves worry since a pony may contract tetanus from a wound so tiny that neither you nor he noticed it. The other preventive measure is required when an unvaccinated pony receives a serious wound. Then a single injection of antitoxin should be given by the vet to give temporary tetanus protection for that wound only.

Worming the Pony
Even the healthy pony requires regular treatment for worms. Every pony has some parasitic worms living internally and their numbers have to be kept down as the microscopic eggs and larvae in the pony's droppings contaminate the pasture, although they are not dangerous to people or farm animals. If a horse or pony picks them up while grazing these develop into more adult worms which in turn shed more eggs and larvae. Huge numbers of such parasites can build up both on the grass and in the pony, whose health may be seriously affected.

Worms are most harmful to young ponies, under five years old. Large numbers can make youngsters thin, anaemic and weak, and may cause sudden illness and death. Older ponies are usually more resistant though they too need regular treatment for worms, otherwise the pasture will become contaminated even if the pony shows no signs of infestation.

Of different types of worm which inhabit the pony's gut, one of the most unpleasant is the 'redworm'. This is in fact a dark grey colour and the adult is about an inch in length. The young worm larvae are microscopic and have a nasty habit (after being swallowed by the pony) of going on a 'tour' round the animal's body. On the way, the tiny worms do considerable damage. This can lead to recurrent bouts of colic in the pony's later life. It can also cause weakness of internal veins and arteries which can lead to their bursting and the pony literally 'dropping dead' – a good reason for keeping worm numbers to the minimum.

Worming a pony is quite simple, especially using the paste preparations in a preloaded syringe that can be squirted easily into the back of the mouth. Other wormers (anthelmintics) come as powders which can be given by the owner in food, (making sure the pony eats it all) or by stomach tube by the vet. Wormers should be varied as worms can become resistant if one drug is used exclusively. Some newer wormers are highly effective, killing migrating worm larvae, and need only be given two or three times a year to adults. Older drugs are only active against mature worms and must be given more frequently (six to eight week intervals in summer). Literature for guidance is available with the drugs, which can be bought from vets.

In recent years, one particular type of worm has received increasing attention. This is the tape-worm, which is extremely common in horses' intestines, and was previously thought to do little or no harm. Tape-worms do not actively burrow into the lining of the intestine, but simply absorb left-over nutrients as the food passes along the alimentary tract. It is for this reason that they were thought to be harmless. There is now good evidence that tape-worms can contribute significantly to the incidence of colic in grazing animals. There is also good evidence that large numbers of tape-worms can cause physical displacement of the bowel, and sometimes even telescoping of one piece of bowel into the other. For this reason, more and more veterinary surgeons are now advising routine treatment to get rid of tape-worms. As tape-worms are picked up at grass, the most logical time of year to do this is when the ponies have finished doing most of their active grazing, i.e. the autumn. Most normal wormers will not eliminate tape-worms, and the most common practice nowadays is to give double the normal dose of one particular type of wormer containing a substance called pyrantel embonate. Your veterinary surgeon will be able to advise you on the actual brand names available for the elimination of tape-worms, and at what dose to administer it.

Not strictly 'worms', but internal parasites none the less, are 'bots'. These creatures have a curious life cycle. The bot itself is a big fat maggot which lives in the pony's stomach, seldom doing any serious harm there. When it is mature, usually in the spring, the bot detaches itself from the stomach lining and passes out with the animal's droppings. Subsequently, it develops into a large fly and the female sticks her little yellow eggs firmly to the pony's fur, usually over the front half of the body. When the pony licks the fur the eggs are taken into his mouth and the whole cycle begins again. Bot eggs can easily be removed from the pony's fur with tweezers, and many worming preparations will also remove bots from the pony's stomach.

A Pony's Dentist
Tooth trouble may interfere with a pony's eating and make him thin and 'poor'. A foal develops a set of temporary 'milk' teeth, just as all mammals do, and these are shed on growing up. When he is adult the pony has permanent teeth, which include a small 'tush' or canine tooth, and generally all this happens without trouble. Occasionally, a pony may develop a small extra 'wolf' tooth just in front of his cheek teeth and if this interferes with the bit it can make a young pony uncomfortable, so that he tosses his head and fights the bit. If this proves a problem then the vet should be asked to come and check the animal's mouth and, if there are any 'wolf' teeth, to remove them.

Most dental problems in ponies arise because the teeth continue to grow throughout the animals' lives. This enables the pony to chew materials as hard as hay and grass without his teeth wearing down short. It also enables us to tell a pony's age from characteristic effects of growth and wear on his teeth.

If a pony's back teeth do not meet exactly, and many don't, they may grow very rough, with sharp points at their edges so that they are not efficient grinders and can cut the inside of the pony's

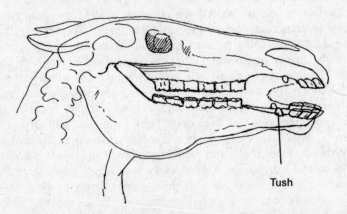

Tush

Fig. 56. The pony's teeth (cut-away view).

mouth. The animal tends to mess with his food and never looks really well, despite generous feeding and proper care. The problem is solved by the vet's rasping down any rough edges at appropriate intervals, usually at least every six months.

Colic

Colic is one of the equine complaints most dreaded by the horse owner. It sounds a simple enough illness – basically a bad stomach ache – but it is more serious than this. A pony is very sensitive to digestive upsets, as has been stressed earlier (Chapters 7 and 8). The most common cause of colic is worm damage, though faulty feeding may be one of several other possible causes. All lead to intense abdominal pain which makes the pony restless and fidgety, with a worried facial expression.

He may pant and sweat and swish his tail, peering occasionally at his flanks. Stamping and kicking at the belly is common, as is pawing the ground before getting down and rolling frantically. It is common for a pony with colic to keep lying down and getting up, because he is suffering intense pain.

Most colic is produced by distension of the intestine for one reason or another. This distension causes pain. The distension can be of gas, typically following injudicious feeding, or a pony 'gutting' itself on, for instance, fallen apples. The gas balloons the intestine causing pain, and the pain has to be controlled until the gas passes along the alimentary tract, and escapes from the rear end. This is known as 'flatulent colic'. The distension may also be produced by food accumulating within the intestine because the intestine itself has become displaced. There are many metres of intestine coiled up in a pony's abdomen, and it is not uncommon for some of this intestine to become displaced to abnormal position. This has an effect similar to 'wringing off' a string of sausages and prevents the normal ingested material moving along from stomach to anus. The distension of bowel, thus produced, can cause intense pain, and these bowel displacements will often require prompt surgical intervention to save the pony's life.

It is the finding of twisted and displaced intestines in horses that have been affected with colic, which led to the belief that the rolling behaviour which colic produces caused the bowel to twist. We now know that this is not the case: the rolling is the result of

Fig. 57. A pony with colic shows signs of pain, such as swishing the tail, kicking at the belly and rolling, as above, or looking sadly at the flank.

the twisted bowel, not the cause of it. In fact, the reverse may well be true, and rolling exhibited by a horse with colic may have some survival value. It is now a common treatment, for some types of displaced bowel, for the horse to be rolled, under anaesthesia from side to side, in order to return the bowel to its normal position. In this way, many cases of what were previously described as surgical colic can now be cured. Perhaps the first horses in the wild that evolved the rolling behaviour in response to pain showed increased survival from some of these bowel displacements, causing the behaviour pattern to become more widespread in the population.

The final reason why the bowel may become distended is because of impaction of faeces. The large colon narrows down significantly as it heads towards the rectum and anus of the pony. The slushy contents of the large bowel gradually have water drawn from them to form the small faecal balls, which are visible within a normal horse dropping. These small balls are produced, one at a time, and accumulate in the rectum, until they are passed as a normal dropping. If the large bowel becomes filled with dense indigestible fibre, it tends to stick fast. This allows the continuous withdrawal of water over a period of time longer than is normal, producing hard, dry faeces. This, in turn, produces a blockage to the large colon causing discomfort.

Ponies affected with impaction colic will often lie still, and roll onto their backs, in order to take the weight of the distended colon off the supporting ligaments which hang from the top of the abdomen. They will try to lie down and lie still for long periods of time. They will usually leave their short feed, but paradoxically will continue to try to eat hay, making the impaction even more of a problem.

The most common reasons for impaction colic are horses receiving insufficient exercise, and being bedded on straw. This combination leads to boredom, which causes the pony to nibble the straw bedding in between its hay feeds. Straw is basically indigestible and causes the blockage within the large intestines. Impactions require immediate treatment by your veterinary surgeon if further important consequences are to be avoided.

So, if a pony has colic, what to do? There is really no question. Get the vet as soon as possible; time spent trying to dose the

animal with colic drinks and home-made remedies is valuable
time wasted. While waiting for the vet to arrive it helps if you
walk the pony about continually to prevent his writhing and
rolling on the ground. If it is cold, put a rug on the animal. A very
deeply bedded stable should also be prepared, preferably with a
light for the vet to work by if it is night-time. When the vet comes
all you can do is follow his instructions to the letter, and hope for
the best. Try, with his help, to work out what could have caused
the colic, so that it can be prevented in future.

Coughs and Colds

'Coughs and sneezes spread diseases' is true of ponies as well as
of people. Ponies suffer from their own version of influenza
which is very infectious, spreading directly or via contaminated
stables, horse boxes and so on. After catching flu the incubation
period is between four days and a week. Then the animal begins
to lose his appetite, develops a fever (that is, feels shivery and
'hot-and-cold') and is miserable, with a runny nose. A cough
develops, and it is most important not to ride a pony while he is
coughing. Any exertion during this period increases the risk of
permanent damage to his lungs, and a cough which could last for
life.

Rest is essential for a pony with influenza. There should also be
somewhere warm to sleep at night, as free from dust as possible.
It is sensible to ask the vet to visit any pony which has signs of
flu.

Influenza is one of the few viral diseases that can be prevented
in the horse by vaccination. The vaccine is given in two doses, a
month apart initially, and then every six months to a year subsequently. Although the manufacturers recommend annual boosting
only, most people have come to realise the protection from the
vaccine is unlikely to last longer than six to eight months. Six
monthly vaccination will prevent severe symptoms from arising
should your pony contact influenza, and is well worthwhile considering. Annual vaccination is often a requirement for ponies
visiting Pony Club camps, when these are held in premises which
may also host thoroughbred horses, such as racecourse stables,
sales rings, etc.

Vaccination does not prevent infection of your pony by other viruses, such as the rhinoviruses. Rhinovirus causes the common cold in humans, and a similar virus is responsible for a similar syndrome in horses and ponies. No vaccination is yet possible against rhinoviruses in any species, because the viruses have a habit of changing rapidly in a very short space of time. By the time a vaccine is developed, the virus has already evolved into a new form, for which the original vaccine would not give protection. Basic nursing care and a short holiday is the only answer once a pony becomes infected.

Another common cause of coughing in ponies was formerly called 'broken wind'. This is not infectious but is due to an allergy which certain individual ponies have to mould spores in hay and bedding. It is now more commonly known as Chronic Obstructive Pulmonary Disease (COPD) because the allergy causes chronic lung damage. Horses with this complaint have a harsh dry cough, which is often heard in the stable or at the beginning of a ride, and no nasal discharge. The lung airway obstruction can be severe, and the animal may be very 'wheezy'. COPD was also called 'Heaves' – from the intense effort such animals have to make to breathe. A so-called 'heaves line', on the chest wall, is due to abnormal enlargement of breathing muscles.

Similar to human asthma, the allergy cannot be cured but can be prevented. Ponies with this problem improve remarkably if turned out all the time. If stabled, hay and straw should be avoided where possible. Fresh shavings or peat bedding are best, and a diet of horse cubes, formulated to give a complete ration, may be fed. Alternatively, soaking hay, in a hay-net, in water for five minutes prevents the spores becoming airborne.

There are some drugs available that will help reduce the severity of symptoms when your pony contacts the allergy triggering dust particles. One of these, Clenbuterol, is the same drug used in many inhalers utilised in human asthma. This is available in a liquid form or powdered granules, for incorporation in the feed. There is also an injection available for use by your veterinary surgeon in the face of any emergency asthmatic attacks your pony may suffer. As well as these drugs, which control the severity of the allergic respiratory disease, there is a range of other drugs, not actually licensed for use in the horse, but derived from drugs used in human medicine, which can be administered in aerosol form via a face mask. This is known as nebulisation. Some of these drugs are designed to prevent the allergic reaction actually taking place when the pony is unavoidably exposed to dust challenges. For instance, a pony that is maintained dust free could be treated by an anti-allergy nebulisation prior to visiting a show or Pony Club camp where other ponies may be using dusty hay which cannot be avoided. If your pony is known to suffer from COPD, then it is worthwhile discussing all the possible alternatives for treatment and control with your veterinary surgeon.

The respiratory infection known as 'strangles' is transmitted by contact with other animals which have the disease, or equipment and buildings they have touched. A pony with strangles looks, and no doubt feels, ill, with a fever and no appetite. Characteristic swellings, which sometimes interfere with breathing, develop on either side of the animal's throat, and a nasty white discharge runs from his nose.

Prompt treatment from the vet is important, though with modern drugs it is not the killing disease it was. Careful nursing is also necessary, and the pony will appreciate a warm stable with a thick bed. Rugs and stable bandages may also be needed to prevent him from getting cold. Wash away dried discharge from his eyes and nose with warm water and drying the area afterwards with cotton

Fig. 58. A pony with strangles looks ill, with no appetite.

wool will also help. Because strangles is very infectious the pony should be isolated from others and grooming tools, rugs and the like – which can carry the infection – should be soaked in disinfectant and washed.

When the pony has recovered, the bedding should be burnt and the stable walls also cleaned with disinfectant. Your own hands and clothes can also carry infection so that it is best to keep an old, washable, coat to wear when you are dealing with an infected pony, and your hands should be washed thoroughly when you have finished.

The strangles organism can survive for a long period of time on woodwork, fences, etc. These often cannot be disinfected, if the pony has been out in a field prior to his diagnosis. For this reason, it is a good idea to treat your premises as infected for at least a month after the last clinical signs have been shown by any horse on the premises.

Skin Disease

Ponies, especially those in poor condition, are occasionally infested with lice. These active little creatures, brown and about one-tenth of an inch long, are most obvious in the mane and tail. They cause itching so that the pony scratches, and may become bald and sore. A wide range of insecticidal drugs is available to remove lice, which are especially found in winter.

The vet should also be asked about the rarer condition known as 'sweet itch' which is an irritation with thickening, baldness and inflammation of skin at the bases of mane and tail. No parasites are visible, and the small number of ponies which are affected only suffer from sweet itch during the summer months. The disease is caused by abnormal sensitivity to the bites of certain midges. It usually disappears if the pony is stabled during the early morning and from late afternoon onwards when the midges are about. The stable must be protected from the possibility of midges following the horse into it. This can be achieved by fitting metal door and window grills, outside which is fitted a conventional mosquito net.

Warts are occasionally a problem with young animals, though true warts seldom affect a pony over five years old. They develop mainly on the pony's muzzle, often in a large, unsightly crop, which is ugly, but within three months they usually disappear suddenly.

Harness galls are not uncommon, arising mainly when ponies have to wear ill-fitting tack. The area of skin which is rubbed becomes sore and thickened and may be quite painful. The first thing to do is to stop riding the pony until the tack can be modified so that it does not chafe the sore place. Treatment with a mild antiseptic ointment may help the gall to heal more quickly.

Saddle sores are one kind of harness gall. The most important treatment is usually to find a saddle which fits the pony properly. The areas covered by the saddle and girth should be checked regularly and kept as free as possible of mud and sweat. A nasty gall may require the attention of the vet.

Ponies that are out all the time in wet weather may develop a condition known as 'Rainscald'. A bacterial infection forms pus under 'paint-brush'-like gatherings of hairs on the back. A similar infection on wet dirty legs is often called 'mud fever'. Removing the scabs with antibacterial shampoo is usually sufficient to treat 'Rainscald'. A soothing ointment will also help 'mud fever'. If the leg swells, the vet must be called to give antibiotic injections. Soothing ointment is also helpful for cracked heels which are also a problem in wet winter weather.

Ringworm is also infrequently found on ponies' skin. Bald non-itchy patches appear, often beginning under the girth. It responds to antifungal treatment, but is very infectious, and care must be taken to keep infected tack or grooming kit away from other ponies.

Azoturia, 'Monday morning disease', 'setfast', or 'tying-up'
These names, in common usage, all refer to a disease which is becoming increasingly common in ponies, the technical name for which is exertional rhabdomyolysis. This poorly understood disease produces very painful cramping of the muscles of the hind quarters, and the back of the thighs, which develops as exercise progresses. The pony becomes increasingly unwilling to go forwards and will often eventually refuse altogether. Once he stands still, he will scrape the ground, and may sweat and tremble because of the severe pain experienced in the muscles. In extreme cases, the pony may even collapse or try to lie down and roll as if suffering from colic.

Although most cases of tying-up are relatively straightforward to deal with, in its most severe form the condition can be life-threatening and is always a cause for concern. Veterinary attention should be sought if the pony is showing extreme pain or unwillingness to move.

When ponies are affected with this disease the muscles of the quarters and along the back of the thighs become hard to the touch and the pony will show a marked pain response if the muscles are prodded. It is probably unwise to force the pony to move, but, in extreme cases, if the episode of setfast or tying-up happens during a ride, then it is permissible to walk slowly home. If he refuses, then help should be sought and a horsebox or trailer called for to transport the pony home. A veterinary surgeon will probably want to administer a pain killing drug, and may even suggest intra-venous fluids in severe cases.

The causes for setfast are not well understood. The incidence seems to have increased with the growing popularity of Arabs and Arab crossbred ponies, and the prevalence of the tendency to over-feed and under-work native pony breeds. Whilst the causes of an individual attack are not well understood, the attacks almost always happen because of a change in the exercise regime of the pony. Tying-up appears to be a problem related to the storage of excessive energy by the pony, usually because of a combination of over-feeding and irregular exercise. Although there are no hard and fast rules to prevent all cases of this affliction, the following guidelines will help in almost all cases.

1. Try to ensure that your pony receives the same amount of exercise each day; the pony most at risk is the 'weekend pony', which receives scant attention during the week but is tacked up and ridden hard on Saturday and Sunday.

2. Try to ensure that your pony spends the least hours possible in the stable during the day and is turned out, even if only in a small courtyard, when possible.

3. Avoid over-feeding. As discussed in the nutrition chapter of this book, native ponies really only need hay, grass and water to survive. Whilst the administration of a multi-vitamin/mineral lick or supplement would be an ideal complement, excessive feeding of high-energy feeds, such as oats, maize and barley, are contra-indicated unless the pony is doing sufficient hard work to

need this fuel. Far more problems are caused nowadays by over-feeding of ponies than by under-feeding them.

When you are bringing a pony up into full work, with a view to competing, always try to *follow* your exercise programme with feed rather than feeding ahead of it. In other words, feed your pony for trotting by feeding him as if out of work. When he starts to canter, feed him with sufficient food to trot only. Only when you are ready for full work, step up his feeding regime to a full complement of high-energy feeds.

Monday morning disease received its name in times gone by because of the tendency of working plough-horses to develop the syndrome, having had a day off on Sunday. If your pony is prone to tying-up, then don't give him a day off!

The Pony's Sex Life
Ponies, like horses, breed during only part of the year. A mare comes into 'season' and is receptive to the stallion for four to six days in every twenty-one. While she is in season the mare may be more flighty than usual, and show an unusual interest in other ponies. The first 'season' of the year is usually sometime in March and then they continue regularly until September, though animals differ greatly one from another.

Mares breed until they are quite old and extra risks attached to an elderly animal having a foal do not appear to be very great. The mare is sent to the stallion to be mated or 'covered' for which the owner usually charges a stud fee. He may also ask that the mare be 'swabbed' by the veterinary surgeon to check that she has no infection which she could pass on to the stallion. The gestation period, between mating and foaling, is about 336 days and the mare can be tested by the vet to see if she is in fact pregnant. If she is, she should not be worked later than about six months before she is due to foal, and thereafter should be fed well.

A novice pony owner would probably be best advised to send the mare to a stud, where foaling can be supervised by someone experienced. If the mare is to foal at home it is generally best to let her foal on her own in a clean paddock if the weather is good, or a large, well-bedded, loose box if it is bad. The less interference the better during the actual foaling, which is usually quite brisk. Most foals are on their feet and sucking within 2–3 hours of birth.

The all too common recommendations for the pony owner to rush in and sever the foal's umbilical cord are quite wrong. It is via this cord, actually a vein, that the foal receives a large transfusion of blood; it will break in due course, and is best left alone.

A filly (female) foal is allowed to grow up without further veterinary attention, apart from regular worming and vaccination against tetanus and flu. A colt foal will require castration unless he is to be kept for breeding. An uncastrated pony, that is a stallion, tends to be difficult to control and unsafe for normal riding. A colt can be castrated either as a foal, between about fifteen and twenty-four weeks of age, or when he is between a year and eighteen months old. The operation is performed by the vet.

The term 'rig' is used to describe male horses that have one or both testicles retained in the abdomen, and are thus unable to be castrated in the normal way. They are normally infertile but retain some of the sexy ideas of the stallion. They tend to be even more unreliable and bad tempered than 'entires' (stallions), and can be very dangerous. By means of a fairly major surgical operation many of these animals can be made into proper geldings, and then they behave as such.

It is a moot point whether a gelding is preferable to a mare for general riding and driving, and which one chooses is probably primarily a matter of personal opinion. There appears to be little basic difference in temperament, strength or tendency towards disease, although a gelding which has been allowed to grow up to two years or more as a stallion and then castrated will tend to be a little larger and stronger than a mare of the same parentage. Some people maintain that because of her periodic seasons a mare is less reliable than a gelding for riding; and particularly for competitions, where it is important that she should always give of her best, this could be a disadvantage. On the other hand, it is suggested by some that a mare is more responsive as a pet. A gelding has the disadvantage that if he becomes lame and chronically unfit for riding his useful life is then at an end, whereas a mare may be used for breeding, provided of course that other circumstances – such as time, skill and suitable accommodation – are also available. For most people selecting a pony for themselves the decision as to whether it should be mare or gelding becomes a minor one compared with whether it meets other requirements.

14

THE FEET AND LEGS

'No foot, no 'oss' is an old saying. Things haven't changed – a lame pony is still a useless pony. The pony's legs and feet have to carry a very large weight, considering how small are the hooves and how slender are even the coarsest of equine legs compared with the size of the whole animal. This increases the speed and agility of the pony, but means that the feet and legs are highly stressed. However, they are surprisingly tough and ponies in the natural state seldom suffer from lameness.

The situation changes, however, when we 'civilise' the pony. We expect work on a variety of different surfaces, for long periods, so that the pony may get tired and clumsy, and at faster speeds than those at which a wild animal would normally travel. The tame pony also has the extra weight of a rider. In addition to all this we expect the pony to work on hard roads, so, to protect the horn of the hooves, we nail iron shoes to the feet. These are bound to have some effect on the natural functioning of the hoof. How great the effect is depends on how well the shoeing is done, for the aim of a good farrier is to make the shoe interfere with nature as little as possible.

The Foot Itself
The 'hoof' which you see when the pony's foot is on the ground is actually the 'wall' of the foot, the outer casing of tough, horny material. This is similar to, but much stronger than, a human finger or toe nail. The wall grows downwards continually from the top of the hoof, the region where fur gives way to the fleshy 'coronet band'. The front part of the wall of the hoof is called the 'toe', the side parts the 'quarters' and the hind part of the wall is the 'heel'.

The outer layers of the wall of the hoof are insensitive, so that

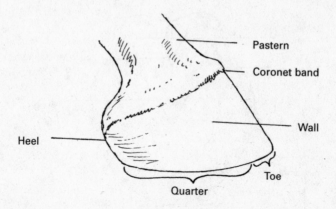

Pastern

Coronet band

Wall

Heel

Toe

Quarter

Fig. 59. The foot.

they can be trimmed and have nails driven through them without causing the pony pain. On its inner side, however, the horn of the wall interleaves with about five hundred vertical folds of sensitive tissue, the 'laminae'. These nourish the wall and attach it firmly to the structures inside the hoof. A nail driven too deeply will penetrate this layer and be felt by the pony. This is likely to lead to the accumulation of pus in the area which – in the confined space of the hoof – is very painful. A pony unfortunate enough to have suffered this is said to have been 'pricked', and will usually require quite lengthy treatment from the vet and a long rest before being fit for work again. This is one of the main reasons it is illegal for anyone other than a properly trained farrier to try to shoe a pony.

The outer surface of the wall is shiny. This is due to a very thin layer of an almost varnish-like waterproof material produced by the coronet band. It is very important because it prevents the horn of the wall from drying out, which would make it brittle and inflexible. Removing this waterproof layer by rasping any but the very bottom part of the wall during shoeing is therefore very damaging to the hoof.

If you pick up the pony's hoof you will see that most of the under-surface is of a slightly flaky-looking horn. This is the 'sole', which also grows continually though it is kept to its proper thickness by the flakes of horn falling off. This happens whether or not the pony is shod. The sole should never be pared, nor any but the

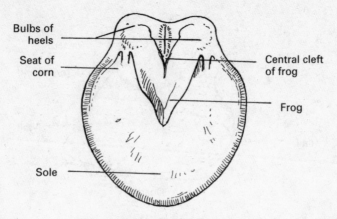

Bulbs of
heels

Seat of
corn

Central cleft
of frog

Frog

Sole

Fig. 60. The underside of the hoof.

very loose flakes removed. It is this layer of horn which protects
the pony's foot which treads on, for example, a stone, just as the
skin of the sole of your own foot gives protection if you walk
barefoot over pebbles.

In the middle of the underside of the foot is a V-shaped piece
of more leathery horn. This is the 'frog' which is softer and more
sensitive to pressure than the horn of the sole or wall. The frog has
several functions. Firstly, being sensitive, it lets the pony know
whether the hoof has actually touched the ground, as the heel normally hits the ground fractionally before the toe.

Secondly, it acts as an anti-slip device – and is better than
almost any man-made one.

Thirdly, the frog is most important in reducing concussion as
directly beneath it lies the 'digital cushion', a pad of fatty fibrous
tissue which acts as a shock-absorber. This pad is responsible for
the last function of the frog, which is to pump blood round the
foot. Whenever the pony puts weight on the foot (provided the
frog touches the ground) the digital cushion is squeezed and, like
a sponge, forces blood out through the veins of the foot. This last
function is very important as the foot is some distance from the
pony's heart so the circulation may be poor.

It is noticeable that many ponies, if made to stand still for very
long periods, will develop slightly 'filled' or swollen legs. This
happens because the circulation to feet and legs is not being

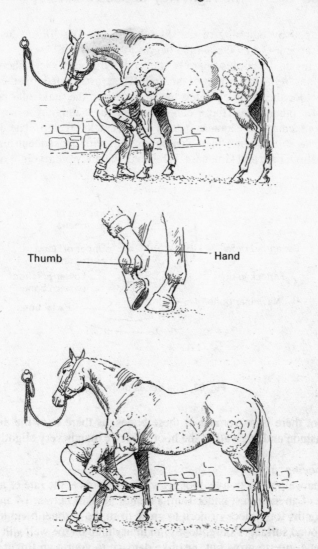

Fig. 61. Picking up a pony's foot.
Standing close to the pony, run your hand down the leg (top). As you press gently on the back of the fetlock, the pony will probably lift the foot. Hold the foot firmly. A pony reluctant to lift the foot can probably be encouraged if you press your finger and thumb on either side of the tendons just above the fetlock.

helped by pumping of the digital cushion. The 'filling' usually disappears when the animal begins to walk about.

Inside the hoof is, literally, the 'end of the pony's leg', the small bones of the lower part of the limb. These are jointed together and include the relatively large 'pedal bone' and the 'navicular bone'. Like other bones these can suffer fractures ranging in severity from complete shattering to a small crack or chip. The joints between the bones may also be injured, with consequent inflammation, pain and lameness. Whenever the pony puts weight on the

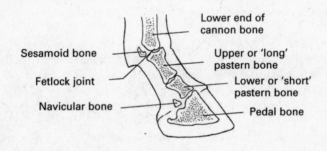

Fig. 62. The bones of the foot.

foot there is movement of these bones, as there is of the digital cushion and the wall of the hoof, which expands very slightly.

Shoeing the Pony

The wall of the pony's foot grows downwards at the rate of about ⅜ of an inch (just under 1cm) a month. It takes between 4 and 12 months for a piece of horn to grow from the coronet band to the ground surface. Consequently, an injury high on the wall will take some time to grow out, just like damage to your own finger nail. But even though the pony's hoof grows continually this will not keep up with the wear which results from trotting on tarmac roads, or even hard-baked or rocky earth. To prevent the horn being worn back until the pony is sore, a shoe of iron or steel, or very occasionally plastic, is nailed round the ground surface of the wall.

The nails are driven into the wall at an angle so that they emerge a little way up it and can be cut off to leave little hooks or 'clenches'.

The shoe gives such good protection that the hoof grows without being worn away at all. If shoes are left on for more than four to six weeks, serious distortion of the feet can occur. This is why a farrier should be asked to attend to a pony every four to six weeks to trim them. This applies whether shoes are worn or not. The hooves may be re-shod with the old shoes (a 'remove') or with new ones. A pony without shoes will also require monthly paring of the feet, for confined in a field in Britain, the hooves will not be worn sufficiently to keep them in good shape.

The Farrier's Work
Watch the farrier at work – you will be seeing a highly skilled craftsman, trained over many years, doing a difficult and exacting task. In shoeing a pony the first job is to remove the old shoes. The farrier knocks up the clenches on the wall of the foot, so that he can lever off the shoe with big pincers. You will notice how the special leather apron he wears gives protection when he rests the pony's foot on his knee for this job.

Next, he pares the foot to remove the surplus growth of horn. A special, very sharp, knife is used for this and a rasp – a coarse file – for reducing the part of the wall which is in contact with the shoe (or the ground in an unshod pony). This is called the 'bearing surface' and is rasped to the proper length so that it is completely level. If a pony is to be left unshod, no more is done.

Originally, shoes were made by hand, using the forge to heat them and a hammer and anvil to shape them. Now, most farriers buy shoes which are ready-shaped and have nail holes stamped in them, though they still need to be individually fitted to each hoof. In 'hot shoeing' the shoe is heated so that it is quite malleable and any alterations are made then: a more exact fit can be obtained this way. 'Cold shoeing' is done without the help of the forge and a good fit is harder to achieve as the cold metal is so much more difficult to work. Hot shoeing is therefore to be preferred if available, though as farriers become fewer there may be no choice in the matter.

The shoe is fitted approximately to the pony's foot before it is

Fig. 63. The farrier tamping down new clenches. He has a special
leather apron.

'burnt on', that is, the hot shoe is held in place on the hoof.
Despite the searing and the clouds of acrid smoke, few ponies
object to the burning on because they cannot feel the heat unless
the hoof has been very badly pared. While the hot shoe is held to
the hoof any slight discrepancies in fit become obvious and slight
alterations can be made. The shoe should always be made to fit
the hoof but it tends inevitably to be the other way round with cold
shoeing.

Next, the shoe is cooled and the ends of heels filed smooth.
Then it is nailed on with horse-shoe nails of special, high quality,
metal. The number of nails per shoe is kept to a minimum which
depends on the size of the foot – five, six or seven being enough
for most ponies. The nails are directed through the wall, and
guided accurately by sound, feel and skill. The points are twisted
off and the clenches finished neatly so that they look like small
squares of metal in the horn of the wall.

A shoe is rather more than a simple semi-circle of iron. Most
shoes have a small 'clip' of metal turned up at the toe, or on hind
shoes, two 'quarter clips', one on each side of the toe. The clips
help to keep the shoe in position and prevent its being dragged
backwards. The shoe also has a groove, known as a 'fuller', running along the ground surface, which helps to give a good grip.
'Calkins' were, and still are occasionally, used to improve the

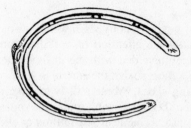

Fig. 64. The shoe, showing nail holes and toe clip.

foothold afforded by a shoe. They are made simply by turning under the metal at the heel to make a small step. More often used now are 'studs' of various types, many of which have specially hardened cores to prevent their wearing right away. These may be of the variety which is knocked into the heel of the shoe by the farrier and which stay in place throughout the life of the shoe, or they may screw into a special threaded hole. This second type, often called 'screws', is more frequently used for ponies competing in jumping and gymkhana events where they will not be required to go on the road. Then a larger stud can be used as it sinks into the soft ground.

The stud is screwed in, usually on the outer heel of each foot, before the competition. The hole in the shoe is normally filled with a plug of tow or metal to prevent it accumulating dirt. This is removed and the thread cleaned with a tap before the stud is screwed in with a spanner. After the event the studs are removed and the plug replaced.

Another anti-slip device, not used so much nowadays, is 'frost nails'. These are special horse-shoe nails with pointed heads which were put in place of the ordinary flat-headed nails when the roads became icy and slippery. They were used for working animals, such as vanhorses, which had to go out whatever the weather. They are very seldom used on modern ponies because, if the roads are icy, few people would consider riding for pleasure. Incidentally, if you do wish to ride in snow, the danger is that the snow 'balls' into big icy lumps in the pony's feet. This is prevented by liberally smearing thick engine grease over the sole periodically during the ride.

Against Shoeing

The aspect of having a pony shod which no-one likes is its cost, but unavoidably the attention of a skilled farrier is expensive. Another problem avoided with the unshod pony is that of 'casting' or losing a shoe, so that the animal is walking unevenly on the three remaining shoes. Worse still is to have one hanging by a single nail. The shoe may swing round and injure the opposite leg. Loose shoes make a characteristic rattling or clicking sound as the pony goes along the road. They are usually the result of leaving too long an interval between visits to the farrier and are generally the fault of the owner. The tendency of the clenches to rise when the shoes have been on too long should be a useful warning.

If shoeing is done inexpertly, permanent damage to the hoof may result. If the pony is shod so that the frog never touches the ground, even on turf (when the shoe sinks in) the anti-concussion and pumping actions of the digital cushion are largely prevented. In a pony which is regularly and properly shod, the frog is noticeably well-developed and broad at the heels. This indicates that the blood supply to the foot is kept moving every time the hoof is put to the ground. If this does not happen then there is stagnation of the blood supply and the whole foot suffers. It has been suggested that this can predispose the hoof to a number of different types of lameness. If a pony is lame and avoids putting weight on one foot for a long time, that hoof becomes narrow, boxy and 'contracted', with a small wizened frog. The cause is insufficient weight being applied to the digital cushion to make it 'squelch' properly.

In the unshod pony the problem of lack of frog pressure does not arise (the frog is automatically in contact with the ground). Nor does it arise in an animal shod with 'grass tips'. These are effectively the front half of a normal shoe and are used to prevent the toe of the hoof from splitting. Ponies doing only a little road work are sometimes shod with grass 'tips'; unfortunately, these, like conventional shoes, need removing every four to six weeks, representing no great saving. Money can be saved by not having a pony shod, as it is much cheaper only to have the feet trimmed every six weeks or so. Many animals which are ridden infrequently, or very slowly on grass, do not require shoeing, and are probably better without it.

Some injuries may occur during shoeing, though these are

uncommon at the hand of a skilled farrier. The 'prick' or nail driven into the sensitive part of the foot has already been mentioned. Occasionally a shoe may be put on so that it presses on the sole, with bruising of sensitive underlying tissues as a result. 'Corns' or bruises may develop in the 'seat of corn' if the shoe's heel begins to rub there, often because it moves with growth of the hoof. This injury is most frequently the result of leaving shoes on too long.

Lameness

Lameness is the unevenness of gait caused, most frequently, by a pony limping while trying to avoid putting too much weight on a painful leg or foot. It is not possible to miss really obvious lameness as the pony will hobble and be reluctant to move, often holding up the affected limb. Mild lameness is not easy to spot. Fore-leg lameness is the more common, since the front legs bear greater weight and are more likely to be injured. To check for this, trot the pony towards you without a rider and with the leading rein slack, on a hard flat surface (remember that roads have a camber). If lame, the pony will probably show it by nodding the head at every other stride. The head comes down as the sound (unaffected) leg comes to the ground. The pony tries to avoid putting too much weight on the 'hurt' foot. Hind-leg lameness is not easy to detect, but if the pony is trotted away, you will notice that the quarters move unevenly.

Finding the seat or cause of lameness is often very difficult. The vet should be consulted for help and advice, otherwise the lameness may be attributed to quite the wrong cause and the pony rested, possibly for months, pointlessly. Quite often the injured area is detectable by swelling, heat and pain in the region, particularly noticeable if the lame leg is compared with the opposite sound one. Not all lameness originates below the knee and hock, though much of it does. Injuries to the elbow, stifle, shoulder, hip and spine may be responsible, and should not be forgotten.

Riding a lame pony will only make it worse. Rest is therefore most important. With many mild strains and sprains a few days' rest and repeated application of cold water, from a slowly trickling hosepipe, may be enough to effect a cure. If the trouble is

Fig. 65. Obvious lameness is easy to spot.

more persistent the vet should be consulted. If it is suspected that the trouble is in the foot, then have the pony's shoes removed before the vet comes so as to save time and visits.

Lameness may arise for a variety of reasons and in many different areas. Shoeing injuries have already been mentioned, and these are generally mild. A 'prick' which develops into a large abscess in the hoof can, however, do permanent damage and put a pony off work for a very long time. Lameness caused by neglect, such as soreness due to cracked heels and mud fever, is usually temporary, provided it is treated. So is 'thrush', where the frog becomes foul-smelling and oozy. This is usually the result of the pony standing for long periods on dirty, wet, bedding, or from not having the feet picked out regularly. The frog becomes inflamed and sore and the pony is understandably reluctant to work well. Mild cases are simply treated by daily application of Stockholm tar to the frog until it is normal again. More serious cases require veterinary attention.

Some lameness is due to self-inflicted injury, e.g., the pony striking one leg with another, and causing cuts and bruises, as in cases of 'brushing' and 'over-reach'. This usually occurs because the pony is young, unfit, tired or has faulty action. Such animals will require special protection for their legs.

Bandages and Boots

The bandages which are put on an animal for work are quite different from those used in the stable to give warmth. An exercise bandage is usually of stockinette or some other slightly elastic material. It must always have a layer of cotton wool or, even better, gamgee tissue (cotton wool supported by coarse gauze) underneath it. The gamgee tissue is cut so that it covers the pony's leg from just below the knee to just above the fetlock, and it is wrapped round the leg so that it is flat and smooth. The bandaging is started at the upper edge, leaving a frill of about half an inch of cotton wool showing above the bandage, and continued downwards firmly to cover the lower edge of the cotton wool. The bandage is taken up again so that the tapes can be tied neatly on the outside of the pony's cannon bone. Bandages must not be put on, or tied, too tight.

As an alternative to bandages, fitted boots are sometimes used to cover the cannon bone area. These are better for protection from knocks and bangs than for support. The boots are made of leather or fabric with leather re-inforcement over the vulnerable areas – such as the inside of the fetlock. Fastened with straps and buckles on the outside of the leg (straps pointing backwards), the

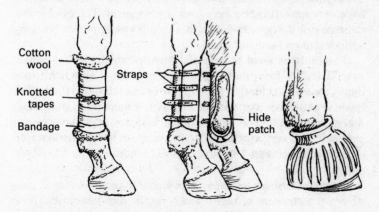

Fig. 66. Bandages and boots.
Exercise bandage (left), boots (middle) and over-reach boot (right).

boots need only be tight enough to prevent them slipping down. Care should be taken that grit does not get underneath them and rub the pony's skin.

'Over-reach boots' are occasionally necessary, for some ponies' action is such that they cut the heels of their front feet with the inside rim of the toe of the back shoe. This is particularly likely to happen in very muddy, 'deep', going. The overreach boots are made of rubber which will stretch sufficiently to go over the hoof, and the boot fits round the pastern to cover the endangered area.

Whether or not bandages and boots give worthwhile support to the leg is debatable, though they are quite often put on horses and ponies for this purpose. A very wide variety of injuries to the bones and tendons of the leg, especially the lower leg, are possible, and a description of each one is really beyond the scope of this book.

Some of these injuries are more common than others, and some are also avoidable. 'Splints', for example, are bony lumps which develop on a pony's cannon bone. They only affect young animals and are the result of working an immature pony whose bones are not fully developed. Repeated jarring causes minute fractures in the splint bones on the inside edge of the cannon in the forelegs below the knee. These are painful and make the pony lame. Though large splints are unsightly they seldom cause lameness once they have finished their own development. The trouble can quite obviously be avoided by not riding young ponies for long periods and on hard surfaces.

'Laminitis' is another type of lameness which is often avoidable. It differs from most other forms in that it affects all four limbs, though it is hard to miss as it is excruciatingly painful. The laminae of all four feet become very hot, inflamed and thickened. A pony with laminitis often lies down, is reluctant to move, or eat, and may look very much like a colic sufferer, though the burning heat of the feet will help to distinguish between the two conditions.

Prompt veterinary treatment is essential to reduce as far as possible the permanent changes which result from laminitis. These may make the pony unfit for anything but light work, if that. After laminitis the hoof becomes deformed, with a 'dropped' or convex sole instead of the normal concave one, and the pony may take to standing noticeably on the heels. With modern treatment an attack of laminitis may be quite brief, but it will still produce 'founder rings', ridges round the wall of the hoof which gradually grow out.

And the cause of laminitis? It is most common in over-fed ponies, which are allowed to stuff themselves with grass when it is at its richest in the early summer. Though laminitis occurs occasionally in ponies already sick for some other reason, obesity is a far more common cause. Laminitis is one of the commonest health problems in ponies, and one that can be prevented. To avoid getting laminitis, it is essential that a pony that tends to be tubby, or has suffered from laminitis previously, should not have access to rich grazing in early summer (it may have to be stabled) and should not be given more than the minimum amount of concentrates at any time of the year.

15

BUYING A PONY

You know you want a pony. You have decided that you can afford to keep one. The next problem is that of purchasing a suitable animal. Of course, anyone can go out and buy a pony, but will it be the right pony for the purpose, and will it be a fair price? Horse-dealing has the justifiable reputation of bringing out a dishonest streak in the most upright of people. Take care not to be misled into paying an exorbitant price for a totally unsuitable animal.

Another problem is the mass of free advice which is offered by self-styled experts; much of this has to be taken with a big pinch of salt. This does not mean that one should not take advice from those more experienced than oneself; far from it, but it is wise to listen to several points of view.

Before embarking on a pony-hunt, decide just what sort of pony is required. This depends greatly on the age and size of the person who is to ride it, as it is on this that the approximate height of the animal will have to depend. A rough guide is that a pony up to 12.2 HH will carry someone twelve years old or less, one between 12.2 and 13.2 HH a rider twelve to fourteen years old, and a pony 13.2 to 14.2 HH a rider up to sixteen years of age; an animal over 14.2 HH (which is technically a horse) will probably be needed for someone bigger than this. For a young rider who is already big for his age ponies rather bigger than the average sizes will be required, as it is better to buy a pony that is a little too large than to purchase one that is rather small and will be rapidly out-grown.

Consider also whether a mare or gelding is wanted. A mare can be kept for breeding when even the youngest member of the family has grown too big to ride her. Geldings, on the other hand, are said to be more reliable in temperament and performance.

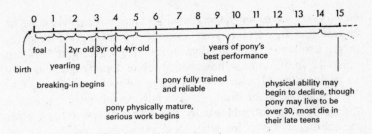

Fig. 67. A pony's life.

A 'First' Pony

After the height range, the next aspect to consider is the use to which the pony will be put. A 'first' pony must above all be absolutely quiet and sweet-tempered. Appearance is not of great importance. Neither is age, though the pony should be well beyond the naughty, adolescent stage. A minimum of six or seven years old is best. Many a first pony can look back over twenty or more years of service to young riders. There is much to be said in favour of such a venerable animal in terms of sense and reliability. Slight physical deterioration due to age may be overlooked, though the vet's opinion should be the deciding factor on such matters.

It is important that a young rider should not be frightened by his or her first pony. One of the most ridiculous situations which arises all too frequently is that the novice rider is given a young pony, sometimes no more than a six-month-old foal, 'so that they can grow up together'. Young ponies are strong and require firm handling and training to make them safe and pleasant to ride. It is hard to see how an inexperienced person, even worse a young child, can be expected to cope with such an animal.

Kind temperament is of paramount importance in the first pony. The next consideration is that of shape. Some ponies, and this applies particularly to Shetlands, are rather broad. This will over-stretch the rider's short legs, and the saddle may slip round the plump barrel. Thirdly, the pony must be safe in traffic, even if unlikely to be ridden on the road except on a leading rein.

A Second Pony

The young rider builds up confidence with a first pony. Inevitably there comes a time when the animal becomes too small and has to be replaced. In a second pony, as with any other, good temperament, gentleness and freedom from vice or naughtiness are essential. In this animal, however, absolute docility is not usually so important and liveliness – so long as it does not amount to taking advantage of the rider – is generally an advantage. It makes the riding more fun and usually means that the pony has greater capabilities as far as jumping, local gymkhanas and the like are concerned.

Quietness in traffic is of course vital in the second pony. This animal will probably be expected to carry an as yet inexperienced rider along the public highway. The animal's age is more important, too, as more strenuous work may be required. Young ponies are best avoided, but generally those between six and twelve years old are well able to do all that is asked of them, provided they are physically fit. Indeed, many older animals also perform well, and have the advantage of being rather cheaper than those in the prime of life.

Cost comes into the picture when deciding what sort of pony is wanted. The animal's age, appearance, breeding and past performance record all play a part in putting the price up or down. Appearance and breeding are also significant in the cost of keeping the pony. A highly bred miniature racehorse will be more expensive to feed and will need to be stabled. A tougher mountain or moorland type pony will live happily in a field with just a shelter and relatively little extra food.

Some ponies are offered for sale as 'specialists' in certain types of work. The 'Junior Jumper' is one such. If the animal has won a few show-jumping competitions the price will increase accordingly. The same applies to the Show Pony, a beautiful creature which, like the jumper, may require very skilful handling and a competent or expert rider. It is easy to over estimate riding ability and it is a false kindness to buy such an animal which will frighten a rider who is unable to cope. Often more fun is to be had from an ordinary pony which could be in turn a hack, a hunter, a trekking pony, a gymkhana winner, or even a driving pony.

Where to look for the Pony
Have a rough picture in mind of the size and weight-carrying

ability, hardiness and age, of the animal wanted, and probably the approximate price. Where do you find a pony for sale? If there is a professional horse dealer in the district he may be the best person to go to. This perhaps seems surprising, but a well-established trader has his reputation to consider, and is unlikely to sell a real 'dud' to someone living locally. Nonetheless, in buying a pony it is for the purchaser to beware. 'Warranties' and promises with regard to the animal have to be treated warily for there is seldom redress unless actual fraud can be proved. This is very seldom possible.

Novices often ask for trouble by going to a dealer and trying to pretend they are expert judges of horse-flesh. To the professional it is of course obvious that they are not. Indeed, though the dealer might try to find an appropriate animal, the know-all may go so far as to sell himself a completely unsuitable horse but, in his 'wisdom', he is impossible to dissuade.

If you know little about buying ponies it is best to admit the fact. Say what type of pony you want and for what purpose, and leave it to the dealer to find something to fit the bill. He will probably charge rather more for it than you might have paid elsewhere, but – provided he is reputable – you will have had the benefit of his experience in picking out a suitable pony. He will probably be willing to give you some help with your new acquisition as well.

An alternative is to buy a pony from a private home. As animals are being outgrown by their young riders all the time, there is a continual stream of children's ponies for sale for this reason. It should not be forgotten, however, that some come on the market because they have been unsatisfactory in other ways. Do not make the error of believing that a private vendor is bound to be honest in dealings with ponies. There are a minority of pony enthusiasts who supplement their incomes by buying in unlikely looking ponies, smartening them up and selling them on as 'family pets – to good homes only'. These animals can be very good performers, though generally a pony that passes from hand to hand does so for good reasons, such as vice, physical weakness, or poor performance.

Ponies are offered for sale in the advertisement columns of many local papers, and in the weekly journal *Horse and Hound*. At the local branch of the Pony Club the Secretary or District

Commissioner may also know of children's ponies for sale and, what is more, also know something of their temperament and performance records. It may take some time to find the right pony. It is certainly very foolish to rush the business and be landed with an animal which is unsuitable for the work required and which may cause you trouble when selling later.

The worst instance of rushing blindly into the purchase of a pony is to buy one at public auction. This is definitely for the experts only. There is seldom opportunity at a sale to give the animal a thorough trial and examination, or for the young rider to consider whether he really likes the pony. Though prices at auction may be low compared with those of a good dealer or a private seller, buying at auction has all too often proved to be false economy.

Looking at the Pony
Going to look at a pony, potentially your own, is always exciting but the prospective owner should not be carried away by the oc-

Fig. 68. Public auctions are for experts only.

casion. The pony has to be sized up carefully, because you decide
on the basis of your own and the vet's examination.

The pony's attitude when approached in the stable will tell a
lot. Is this visitor regarded with friendly interest? Do those gentle
large eyes have a kind expression? Some people scorn those who
consider a pony's facial expression important, but the animal with
the small, 'piggy' eye and a mean look is very often ill-tempered
and 'nappy'. The pony should allow people to walk up and should
show no sign of viciousness or nervousness. If children are to be
carried the pony should not resent handling of the legs or ears, or
picking up of the feet.

The pony's general appearance should be compact, with a
shortish back, sloping quarters and a neck which is neither so long
and 'upside-down' that it looks like a swan's nor so short and
thick that the pony will be able to pull like a train. A pretty head,
with a flat or 'dished' forehead (a bulge between the eyes usually
indicates sour temper, not brains, in horses) and fine features are
desirable. General alertness suggests reasonable intelligence.

Shoulders should be sloping, with withers which carry the

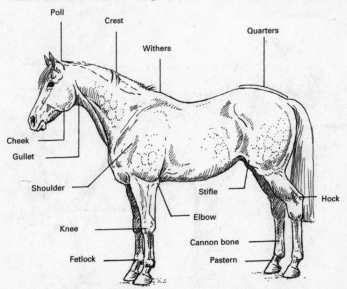

Fig. 69. The points of the pony. The sort to look for.

saddle well. Some ponies are so wide in the back that it is hard to find their withers at all, others are so bony and their withers so high that they are like clothes horses: the happy medium is most desirable. Legs should be straight and strong, which is not the same as the thick heavy tree-trunks of the undersize carthorse. The feet should be round, with broad 'frogs' and a wide open heel; not little narrow boxes which are subject to damage by concussion.

If the overall appearance and demeanour of the pony is pleasant then it should be seen ridden. Usually the vendor provides a rider who will show off the animal's paces and jump it over a fence or two. It is best not to be too impressed by this performance. Bear in mind that some of these young riders are very skilful at getting the best out of a pony and the jumping of fences in the home paddock is frequently well-practised. While the vendor's jockey is riding, note what bit and other tack is being used to control the pony, and, if possible, have it ridden on the road to see its reaction to traffic.

Next the pony should be tried out by the one who may be the

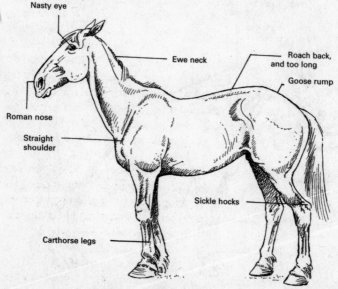

Fig. 70. Not this! The type to avoid.

animal's future rider. Gently walk the pony round the paddock for a few minutes then try a steady trot in circles to right and left. There should be no reluctance on the part of the pony to go either way. There should be no problems over a canter with either right or left leg leading. Try to make your trial ride different from the one given by the owner. Also try to include a specific test to check that the pony will stop obediently when heading for the stables, and that there is no reluctance to turn away from them. If the pony fails this test, it could be the first sign of 'nappiness', a form of rebelliousness hard to cure. Finally, pop the pony over a small fence.

In choosing a pony it is important that the temperament should match that of the rider. A bold young character will enjoy riding a bold pony, while someone who is rather timid will do better on a more stoic animal. This does not mean that any pony should be a 'slug', that is unwilling to take a step unless it is beaten and thumped. Such animals are tedious to ride, and encourage the rider to flap legs and arms like the sails of a windmill in an attempt to make the pony move.

If you consider the pony is suitable there are a few points which should be asked about. Is the pony easy to catch? Are there problems with tying-up, shoeing and clipping? Does the animal walk readily into a horse-box or pony-trailer? The matter of breeding, if it is known, should be considered, and that of height, which can be important in children's ponies. For gymkhanas and most competitive events, the classes are divided on the basis 12.2 HH and under, 12.2 HH to 13.2 HH, and 13.2 HH to 14.2 HH, so that a pony of, say, thirteen hands and two and a half inches is at a disadvantage in having to compete against animals some three inches bigger.

The pony's feeding should also be discussed. It is not unknown for someone to buy a quiet and well-schooled pony and take it home. Within a week the animal has become unmanageable through being fed with unaccustomed oats and other concentrates.

Veterinary Examination
The last consideration is the question of whether the pony is physically fit. This is a matter for your own veterinary surgeon, who examines the animal on your behalf (and at your expense). A

Fig. 71. Measuring a pony.
The height is measured in 'hands' (one hand = four inches) and inches, and is taken from the highest point of the animal's withers. Half an inch is allowed for shoes.

'Vet's Certificate' offered by the vendor is of little value. One of the purposes of the vet's examination is to decide whether the pony is suitable, and fit, for the sort of work you want done. The vendor may have had the animal examined for a quite different use.

You should, of course, tell your veterinary surgeon for what purpose you are buying the pony, as a general purpose child's pony, or as a show pony, for example. Some physical blemishes, such as scars or certain bony enlargements on a pony's legs, make no difference to a pony used for hacking, Pony Club competitions and local gymkhanas. They could, however, seriously affect the chances of a show pony winning a championship event.

The term 'sound' has been deliberately omitted. Though it is widely used by those associated with horses, its meaning is rather woolly. Generally a pony is considered 'sound' if physically fit and having no past or present injuries which affect its capability to perform the work which might reasonably be expected of such an animal. The problem is that there are degrees of 'soundness'.

A horse which is expected to complete a very taxing combined-training three-day-event, or to jump seven feet and more, can have none of the slight signs of wear and tear that would be quite acceptable in a pony which will be asked to do no more than a day's hunting now and then. This is taken into account during the vet's examination of the pony for he could not, and would not, look for superlative physical fitness, nor would he find it in the majority of ponies.

The veterinary surgeon nevertheless makes a thorough examination of a pony on behalf of a prospective purchaser. Any defects found, whether they will affect the pony's performance or not, he notes on the certificate of examination, along with his opinion as to whether or not the pony is a good buy.

If the pony is satisfactory in all respects the final step is to pay, and arrange to get the animal home. Some vendors will deliver the pony, others will suggest the services of a professional carrier to collect the animal. Either way, payment should be made when the pony passes into your care, or that of your agent (the carrier). Unfortunately, in most horse-dealing one has no redress if it is found on getting home, that the pony is not quite what was thought. There is much to be said, therefore, for asking the advice of an experienced horseman when going to look at a pony. This, combined with your own common sense and the vet's opinion, should help in the completion of a fair purchase.

Pony-selling Terms

Some of the terms used by people selling ponies are rather strange, and may need a little explanation. A *patent-safety* pony is docile under all circumstances, and considered suitable for the nervous rider. Such animals tend to be slow, however, and may be very sluggish; or the safeness may be due simply to the fact that the pony is too old or lame to move other than slowly anyway. A point to remember is that the quietest of ponies can become naughty if over-fed, under-worked and consistently spoiled.

A *generous horse, a true christian* or a pony *genuine in every way* means neither that the animal is particularly religious nor that others sold as ponies are in fact camels in disguise. These terms are used to describe the pony's kind temperament and general co-operativeness. Such an animal should have no tendency to

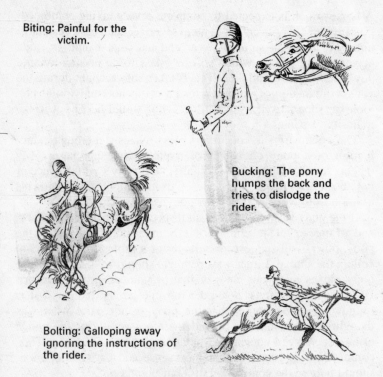

Biting: Painful for the victim.

Bucking: The pony humps the back and tries to dislodge the rider.

Bolting: Galloping away ignoring the instructions of the rider.

Fig. 72. Equine vices to avoid. (i)

rebelliousness.

An animal described as *hot* is one which is inclined to go fast if possible and may run away given the chance. These ponies require skilful riding though many are very good performers despite often having 'mouths of steel'. Such a pony may also be described as *a strong ride* (sometimes a gross understatement) or *not a novice ride*. It is unwise to take on such a pony unless you are a really experienced rider who has kept and ridden quite a variety of animals.

The pony *backed this winter/spring/summer/autumn, lightly backed*, or *ready to school on* is also best avoided unless you have considerable experience in dealing with young ponies. The process of *backing* a pony in this context is getting on the back for the first time; many ponies change hands at this stage in their training. A pony may seem very quiet although it has carried a rider for the first time only a few weeks ago but this is misleading. There is still much to teach such an animal which may become naughty if not handled correctly. These novice ponies are also described as *green* and, occasionally, as *well-broken*. This implies that the training has been carried a little further, though it is not yet complete.

A *quality* pony is generally one whose parents or grandparents include Arab or thoroughbred (TB) horses. This makes the pony a little less sensible, not so hardy and more of a hothead to ride. Not entirely without justification in some cases, such an animal may be described as a *blood pony*. The parentage of a pony is given as (for example) *Cinderella, By Magic Moment* (the father) *out of Pumpkin* (the mother).

An odd term, often given as the reason for selling a pony, is *owner sadly outgrown*. This does not mean that the pony has shot up and is too big for the rider but quite the reverse. Various reasons may be given to explain why a pony is for sale, some genuine, some spurious. An advert may also specify *to good home only*. Often this reflects the vendor's sadness at parting with a well-loved pony. Such people, if genuine, are always pleased to find a good private home for the animal. Be very cautious, however, of becoming involved with those owners who cannot bear to sell and will only loan or lease the pony. Though this may be a financial saving in some ways it can lead to very difficult situations legally. Responsibility for the animal is divided and in case of accident or illness it can be very difficult to decide who should compensate whom. It is better, if possible, to buy an animal, even a cheaper one, outright.

Insurance

Buying a pony and its tack represent a sizeable investment. Accidents and illness may mean extra unforeseen expenses. Insurance is one of the first things to be considered after deciding to buy a new pony. The most important risk to be insured is public liability. This covers the cost of damage to property or vehicles, or injury to other animals or people, caused by the pony getting loose, or kicking out. Many family household insurance

Crib-biting: The pony
gnaws at the manger,
doors, fences etc.

Kicking people: The pony lashes out with the hind legs, usually
unexpectedly.

Kicking the stable:
With front or hind
legs, sometimes just
for impatience, some-
times apparently to
damage.

Napping: The pony would
rather stay at home, or with
other ponies, etc. Evidenced
by refusing to go, or moving
very slowly away from the
stable, but will go as fast as
possible towards it.

Fig. 73. Equine vices to avoid. (ii)

Rearing: Pony stands on hind legs; dangerous as the animal may over-balance and fall on top of rider.

Tearing clothing: A pony chews rug, etc. because of boredom, wrong feeding, dental troubles, being too hot, or just plain mischief.

Weaving: The pony stands at a door or gate, and sways from side to side, getting into a trance.

Wind-sucking: Arching the neck, the pony gulps down air.

Fig. 74. Equine vices to avoid. (iii)

policies include a public liability clause which covers a pony and may also include theft of tack. It is worth checking the 'small print' or phoning the insurance company, and if this is not covered, taking out a separate policy. Ponies can also be insured against death (or destruction on humanitarian grounds), for loss of use, or for vets' fees. 'Loss of use' insurance is more expensive, but can be worthwhile for show ponies, whose value can be greatly reduced through injury. A veterinary examination is usually required by the insurers before 'loss of use' cover is accepted. Mortality and vet fees insurance are relatively inexpensive and are a sensible way of budgeting for unforeseen disasters.

GLOSSARY

Aged. The age of a pony can be told fairly accurately from his teeth until he is fifteen years old; older than this he is described as *aged*.

Arab. A breed of horses imported from North Africa as long ago as the crusades. Being lightly built and fast, strong and sound, with great intelligence and beauty they have been crossed with horses and ponies all over the world to introduce quality to the native stock.

Backing can mean going backwards, but may also describe the business of getting on a young pony's back for the first time.

Bay is a particular colour and describes ponies with brown bodies and muzzles and black manes, tails and legs.

Bit and bitting. Held in the pony's mouth by the bridle the *bit* is essentially a bar of metal used to guide and control the animal. *Bitting* is the training of a young pony to accept and respond to a *bit*.

Black. A pony is described as *black* only if he has a black muzzle as well as a black body, though he may have a few white markings.

Blaze. A broad white stripe down the front of a pony's face.

Breaking-in is training a pony to carry a rider, or draw a carriage, quietly and obediently. This term may be shortened to *breaking*; hence an animal may be described as *broken* or *unbroken*.

Breaking-out can have its customary meaning of escaping from a field or stable, but in horsy parlance it more often means that an animal is beginning to sweat.

Broken knees are knees scarred where the pony has fallen and injured them.

Brown ponies are dark brown in colour with brown muzzles, which distinguishes them from *black* ponies; and brown manes and tails, which distinguishes them from *bays*.

Brushing could indicate grooming, but also describes a fault in the pony's action where he hits one fore or hind leg with the other as he moves; it may also be described as *going close* in front or behind. Boots or bandages may be necessary to protect the animal's lower legs from injury.

Cannon bone. The straight bone which runs from knee or hock to fetlock.

Capped elbow results from repeated bruising of a pony's elbow which causes a large, soft, and ugly, though usually painless, swelling.

Capped hock describes a similar swelling on the hock.

Cast. While lying down a pony may become trapped against a wall or fence so that be cannot get up; he is then described as *cast*. The word is used in a different context in *casting a shoe* which means that the shoe has fallen off the pony's foot.

Chaff is the outermost husk of grain, left on the field by the harvester. It is also hay, cut short (*chop*) and fed to ponies as bulk with their concentrate feed.

Chestnut ponies have ginger-coloured bodies, manes, and tails, possibly with white markings. Ponies whose colour is rather darker, more or less that of cooked liver, are called *liver chestnut*. *Chestnuts* are also the normal horny excrescences on the insides of the pony's legs, above the knee and below the hock.

Cob is a confusing term. To some people, especially saddlers, it describes a size of animal approximately 13.2 to 15 HH. A *cob* may also be just a small and substantial animal, capable of carrying a heavy rider, and from this usage comes the term *cobby*, meaning an animal of sturdy build.

Coloured is sometimes used to describe piebald and skewbald ponies.

Colt. A young male pony which has not been castrated nor used at stud, usually up to three years old; hence a *colt foal*.

Connemara. A breed of ponies native to Ireland and known for their tractability, soundness and intelligence. They are good riding ponies between 13 and 14.2 HH and are most often grey or dun in colour.

Corn means the grain, usually oats, fed to ponies. Animals which are fit and working very hard may need large amounts (though too much will make them frisky), hence the expression *corned up*.

Corns are also the horny, bruised, areas produced by shoes which are left on a pony's feet too long between shoeings.

Curb. A bit acting on the lever principle, tightening a *curb chain* round the pony's lower jaw. A *curb* is also a type of hock injury to which animals with *sickle* shaped, rather than normally angled, hocks are particularly prone.

Dale ponies are native to the North of England, and relatives of the *Fell* breed. About 14.2 HH, the Dale is a strongly built, tractable, utility pony; most are black and all carry 'feathers', or hair, on their heels.

Dartmoor ponies, like the Exmoor, are a breed indigenous to South-West England. Most are under 13 HH, though strong and hardy, and usually bay, black or brown in colour.

Dock. The part of a pony's tail composed of bone, muscle and skin from which grow the long tail hairs. *Docking*, that is removing all or part of the dock, is illegal in the United Kingdom, except where the veterinary surgeon finds that injury to the tail makes it unavoidable.

Dun is a colour, the ponies having honey-coloured bodies with black mane, tail and in many cases black legs too. The name *dun* may also be given to a light brown pony, though such is uncommon.

Eel stripe. A black stripe running along the middle of a pony's back, most often seen on dun animals.

Electric fence. Widely used by farmers, it consists of easily moved insulated sticks, about three feet high, carrying a wire through which is passed a small, intermittent, electric current, generated by a battery unit which makes a loud tick. After one shock animals acquire great respect for the fence.

Exmoor. A tough breed, indigenous to South-West England, Exmoor ponies make good riding animals. About 12.2 to 13 HH they are brown, bay or dun in colour with no trace of white, though a mealy coloured muzzle is characteristic.

Feather is the long hair to be found on the heels of some ponies.

Fell. Once pack animals, this breed was developed to carry panniers of lead from the mines; now it is used for riding and driving. Most are about 13.2 HH, black, dark bay or brown, dun or grey in colour with long curly mane and tail and 'feather' on the heels.

Filly. A young female pony, who has not bred; hence a *filly foal.*

Gelding. A male pony which has been castrated.

Gestation. The period between a mare's being mated, or 'covered,' and her foaling; the average is 336 to 340 days, though considerable variation is quite normal.

Girth. The broad strap which is buckled round a pony to hold the saddle in place.

Grey. Equines are usually described as *grey* rather than white, possibly because ponies are seldom truly white, either because of extraneous dirt or dark hairs in the coat. A *flea-bitten grey* has speckles of grey and brown all over the body while a *dappled grey* has a pewter coloured coat, with lighter areas.

Iron grey describes a more uniform metallic colour, which is very dark in the *grey roan.*

Hacking is simply riding along roads and bridleways, either for pleasure or to get to a particular place.

Hands. A pony is measured in *hands*, one hand being four inches, and height is described as, for example, thirteen *hands* three inches, or 13.3 HH (the HH standing for *Hands High*).

Highland. A breed native to the Highlands and Islands of Scotland, these ponies are strong and docile, ranging in size from about 12.2 to 14.2 HH. The most common colours are dun, brown, black and grey, and many have an eel stripe along their backs.

Horse. This can simply mean an equine of 15 HH or more, or it may be used to describe a stallion rather than a gelding or mare.

In does not indicate fashion, but that a pony is kept *in* a stable, rather than *out* in a field.

Ley (pronounced *lay*) a specially sown mixture of grass and clover, of high value for grazing, and best not ridden over.

Loins. The part of the pony's back between saddle and rump, which is weaker than other areas.

Lungeing. Exercising or training a pony by making him trot, on a long – *lungeing* – rein, in circles round the trainer.

Mare. A female pony which has had a foal, or is over the age of three.

Markings on ponies are usually white and are found mainly on the face and legs; their individual shapes and sizes can be useful for describing and identifying a pony.

Martingales are pieces of harness used to keep a pony's head or reins in the correct position.

Mouth. The pony eats as any other animal, but the mouth also carries the bit and on its sensitivity depends the animal's responsiveness to the rider's signals. A *good mouth* or a *light mouth* is very sensitive, while *a hard mouth* has been injured by rough handling and has little feeling.

Nappy ponies are rebellious and resent leaving their fields or stables, walking slowly, stopping, refusing to go on, etc., on the outward journey but travelling as fast as they are allowed when turned for home.

Native breeds. Some breeds of pony have been, or still are, natural inhabitants of the United Kingdom, appearing wild, though nowadays all are owned by somebody. They are the Connemara, Dale, Dartmoor, Exmoor, Fell, Highland, New Forest, Shetland and Welsh breeds.

New Forest. Coming from the New Forest region of Hampshire, ponies of this breed are usually between 12 and 14 HH, and most are bay or brown. A very good temperament and conformation suitable for riding are usual.

Out is used as an abbreviation for outdoors; *living out* means that the pony is not stabled.

Palomino ponies are a golden colour with white manes and tails.

Piebald is a mixed colour, large patches of black being interspersed with white. Mane and tail may be black or white or parti-coloured.

Pitchfork. A long-handled fork with two slender, sharp prongs, used for moving hay and straw.

Pony. Usually equines of 14.2 HH and under are called *ponies*, though animals used for polo, whatever their size, are also called *ponies*.

Prick. The injury caused by a nail or similar sharp object's being driven through the horn of a pony's hoof into the sensitive part of the foot.

Quidding is the result of soreness of the mouth or teeth which makes the pony 'mess' with food, chewing it slowly and spitting lumps out.

Roan ponies have coats which are an even mixture of white with some other colour. A *blue roan* is black or dark brown plus white, giving a slightly blue appearance; a *red roan* is bay or bay-brown with an admixture of white, while a *strawberry roan* is chestnut with white hairs.

Saddlery sizes. Saddlery is normally sold in three sizes, *pony*, *cob*, and *full size*. *Pony* size will usually fit animals up to about 13.2 HH; *cob* animals from 13.2 to 14.3 HH, and *full size* 15 HH and above. Saddles are measured in inches from front (pommel) to back (cantle) and are designated *narrow*, *medium* or *broad* according to the width of the back of the animal they are intended to fit.

Schooling. Riding a pony to train it, by implication in a marked out arena or *school* in the field.

Shetland. The smallest of Britain's native breeds, the *Shetland* (whose size is usually stated in inches) is often under 40 inches tall. Small and tough, it has great strength of both body and mind.

Skewbald ponies are marked with large patches of white and any colour other than black, usually brown or chestnut. The mane and tail may be parti-coloured.

Snaffle. A type of bit consisting of a straight or jointed bar where contact with the rider's hands, via the reins, is direct rather than through a lever system as it is in the curb.

Snip. A small white marking in the region of the pony's nostrils.

Socks. The name given to/used for legs which are white no higher than the fetlock.

Staling is the term used to describe a pony's urinating.

Stallion. An uncastrated male pony, used at stud.

Star. Any white marking on a pony's forehead may be called a *star*.

Stripe generally means a narrow, white stripe down a pony's face. It has nothing to do with the *eel stripe*.

Stocking is the term sometimes used to describe legs which are white as high as the knee or hock.

Tack. Bridle and saddle are sometimes referred to as *tack*, hence harnessing may be called *tacking up*.

Thoroughbred or *'TB'*. The English Thoroughbred is a breed which has been evolved by centuries of crossing imported, mainly Arab, stock with native animals to produce the fast, athletic, beautiful and sometimes rather highly strung animals we see on modern racecourses. The Thoroughbred has been used to introduce some of its size and *quality,* that is, its lightness of body, speed and activity, to the progeny of TB-native pony crosses.

Vice. A bad habit acquired by a pony, such as persistent kicking in the stable, or biting. A *vicious pony* is one which has a vice that entails deliberately injuring humans or other animals, such as lashing out at them with the hind feet, or chasing people in the field.

Wall eye. An eye which is pink or blue, rather than the more normal dark brown colour.

Welsh ponies are indigenous to the British Isles, and the breed is noted for its attractive appearance and pleasant temperament. Welsh ponies are excellent for riding, with the most common colours grey, dun, cream and chestnut. *Welsh cobs*, which are derived from the Welsh Mountain pony, are larger animals, up to 15.2 HH, and strong, with fine knee action at the trot. This breed is popular for both driving and riding.

Zebra marks. Vertical stripes, usually rather pale, on the pony's neck, limbs or the upper part of his body.

INDEX

(See also Glossary)

RIGHT WAY
PUBLISHING POLICY

HOW WE SELECT TITLES

RIGHT WAY consider carefully every deserving manuscript. Where
an author is an authority on his subject but an inexperienced writer,
we provide first-class editorial help. The standards we set make sure
that every **RIGHT WAY** book is practical, easy to understand,
concise, informative and delightful to read. Our specialist artists are
skilled at creating simple illustrations which augment the text
wherever necessary.

CONSISTENT QUALITY

At every reprint our books are updated where appropriate, giving our
authors the opportunity to include new information.

FAST DELIVERY

We sell **RIGHT WAY** books to the best bookshops throughout the
world. It may be that your bookseller has run out of stock of a
particular title. If so, he can order more from us at any time – we have
a fine reputation for "same day" despatch, and we supply any order,
however small (even a single copy), to any bookseller who has an
account with us. We prefer you to buy from your bookseller, as this
reminds him of the strong underlying public demand for **RIGHT
WAY** books. Readers who live in remote places, or who are house-
bound, or whose local bookseller is unco-operative, can order direct
from us by post.

FREE

If you would like an up-to-date list of all **RIGHT WAY** titles cur-
rently available, send a stamped self-addressed envelope to
ELLIOT RIGHT WAY BOOKS, BRIGHTON ROAD,
LOWER KINGSWOOD, TADWORTH, SURREY, KT20 6TD,U.K.
or visit our web site at www.right-way.co.uk